FIREKEEPER

SELECTED POEMS

T0106676

BY PATTIANN ROGERS

The Expectations of Light
The Tattooed Lady in the Garden
Legendary Performance
Splitting and Binding
Geocentric
Firekeeper: New and Selected Poems
Eating Bread and Honey
A Covenant of Seasons
The Dream of the Marsh Wren:
    Writing As Reciprocal Creation
Song of the World Becoming:
    New and Collected Poems, 1981–2001
Generations

FIREKEEPER

SELECTED POEMS

REVISED AND EXPANDED

PATTIANN ROGERS

MILKWEED EDITIONS

Published 2005 by Milkweed Editions
Cover design by Christian Fünfhausen
Author photo by John R. Rogers
Interior design by Christian Fünfhausen
The text of this book is set in Requiem Text HTF Roman
19 20 21 22 23   5 4 3 2
First Edition

Milkweed Editions, a nonprofit publisher, gratefully acknowledges sup-
port from Anonymous; Emilie and Henry Buchwald; Bush Foundation;
Patrick and Aimee Butler Family Foundation; Cargill Value
Investment; Timothy and Tara Clark Family Charitable Fund;
Dougherty Family Foundation; Ecolab Foundation; General Mills
Foundation; Kathleen Jones; D. K. Light; McKnight Foundation; a
grant from the Minnesota State Arts Board, through an appropriation
by the Minnesota State Legislature, a grant from the National
Endowment for the Arts, and private funders; Sheila C. Morgan; Laura
Jane Musser Fund; an award from the National Endowment for the
Arts, which believes that a great nation deserves great art; Navarre
Corporation Debbie Reynolds; Cynthia and Stephen Snyder; St. Paul
Travelers Foundation; Ellen and Sheldon Sturgis; Surdna Foundation;
Target Foundation; Gertrude Sexton Thompson Charitable Trust
(George R. A. Johnson, Trustee); James R. Thorpe Foundation; Toro
Foundation; Weyerhaeuser Family Foundation; and Xcel Energy
Foundation.

Library of Congress Cataloging-in-Publication Data

Rogers, Pattiann, 1940
   Firekeeper : selected poems / Pattiann Rogers.--Rev. and expanded.
      p. cm.
   ISBN-13: 978-1-57131-421-5 (pbk. : alk. paper)
   ISBN-10: 1-57131-421-0 (pbk. : alk. paper)
   I. Title.
   PS3568.O454F57 2005
   811'.54--dc22   2005008406

This book is printed on acid-free paper.

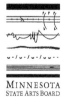

MINNESOTA
STATE ARTS BOARD

FOR EMILIE BUCHWALD
AND H. EMERSON BLAKE

FIREKEEPER: SELECTED POEMS

FROM
GEOCENTRIC (1993)

FROM
OLD SPIRAL OF CONCEPTION (1994)

FROM
EATING BREAD AND HONEY (1997)

FROM
A COVENANT OF SEASONS (1998)

FIREKEEPER

SELECTED POEMS

FROM

THE EXPECTATIONS OF LIGHT (1981)

HIRING THE MAN WHO BUILDS FIRES
FOR A LIVING

He comes when I ask him, during the last half hour
Of evening, begins with his earthen circles,
His rings of rock. Infuriating swagger,
He carries about him the distinct odor of mitigating humus.

But he knows his business. He disappears again and again
Into the trees, taken as if the forest knew him personally,
And comes back always from another direction, his arms
Full of branches having fallen themselves
From great heights without wings nights ago.

When the trees are not totally black, not yet fully entrenched
In the grey sky, imagine how he kneels down
And bends close, how he proceeds with the arrangement.
What is it he believes about this altar? He lays
Each stick religiously as if it had grown
Toward this place from the beginning. What is he whispering
To those dried-up leaves as if they had souls?
There's a blessing here he definitely finds amusing.

I can never see at this point what it is he moves
With his hands or how he concentrates on molding
The invisible as if he could manipulate prophecy, shape

4

The promise to fit the gift to come. Perfect sculptor,
He knows his element thoroughly.

Watching the deep blue curtains as they fall constantly now
Among the dark trees, I admit
He knows with his breath how to make flame live.

And in the midst of it all, what can I think of a man
Who has created in this black forest tonight
A popping circus of blue-gold brilliance plummeting
With such acrobatic radiance that I laugh out loud myself?
Well, I hired him on faith. He was obliged to be
More than I expected.

.   .   .   .   .

IN ORDER TO PERCEIVE

At first you see nothing. The experience is similar
To opening your eyes wide as white marbles
Inside the deepest cave, beneath tons of limestone,
Or being awake in a dark room, your head
Under a heavy blanket.

Then someone suggests there is a single candle
Wavering far off in one corner, flickering red.
You think you see it
As someone else draws your attention to the sharp
Beaming wing tips, the white end of the beak,
The obvious three points of the wild goose overhead
And the seven-starred poinsettia to the west, the bright
Cluster at its belly.

You are able to recognize, when you are shown,
The sparks flying from the mane of the black stallion,
The lightning of his hooves as he rears,

And in the background a thick forest spreading
To the east, each leaf a distinct pinprick of light.

Then you begin to notice things for yourself,
A line of torches curving along a black valley,
A sparkling flower, no bigger than a snowflake,
Shining by itself in the northwest coordinate.
It is you who discovers the particular flash
Of each tooth inside the bear's open mouth and the miners
With their lighted helmets rising in a row.

How clear and explicit, you tell someone with confidence,
That ship, each separate gleaming line of its rigging,
The glowing dots of the oars, the radiating
Eyes of the figure on the prow, the corners
Of each sail lit.

Soon there is no hesitation to the breadth
Of your discoveries. Until one night during the long
Intensity of your observation, you look so perfectly
That you finally see yourself, off in the distance
Among the glittering hounds and hunters, beside the white
Shadows of the swans. There are points of fire
At your fingertips, a brilliance at the junctures
Of your bones. You watch yourself floating,
Your heels in their orbits, your hair spreading
Like a phosphorescent cloud, as you rise slowly,
A skeleton of glass beads, above the black desert,
Over the lanterned hillsides and on out through the hollow
Stretching directly overhead.

Suppose his body was the meticulous layering
Of graduated down which you studied early,
Rows of feathers increasing in size to the hard-splayed
Wine-gloss tips of his outer edges.

Suppose, before you could speak, you watched
The slow spread of his wing over and over,
The appearance of that invisible appendage,
The unfolding transformation of his body to the airborne.
And you followed his departure again and again,
Learning to distinguish the red microbe of his being
Far into the line of the horizon.

Then today you might be the only one able to see
The breast of a single red bloom
Five miles away across an open field.
The modification of your eye might have enabled you
To spot a red moth hanging on an oak branch
In the exact center of the Aurorean Forest.
And you could define for us, "hearing red in the air,"
As you predict the day pollen from the poppy
Will blow in from the valley.

Naturally you would picture your faith arranged
In filamented principles moving from pink
To crimson at the final quill. And the red tremble
Of your dream you might explain as the shimmer
Of his back lost over the sea at dawn.
Your sudden visions you might interpret as the uncreasing
Of heaven, the bones of the sky spread,
The conceptualized wing of the mind untangling.

Imagine the intensity of your revelation
The night the entire body of a star turns red

And you watch it as it rushes in flames
Across the black, down into the hills.

If your father was a redbird,
Then you would be obligated to try to understand
What it is you recognize in the sun
As you study it again this evening
Pulling itself and the sky in dark red
Over the edge of the earth.

.   .   .   .   .

THE RITES OF PASSAGE

The inner cell of each frog egg laid today
In these still open waters is surrounded
By melanin pigment, by a jelly capsule
Acting as cushion to the falling of the surf,
As buffer to the loud crow-calling
Coming from the cleared forests to the north.

At 77 degrees the single cell cleaves in 90 minutes,
Then cleaves again and in five hours forms the hollow
Ball of the blastula. In the dark, 18 hours later,
Even as a shuffle in the grass moves the shadows
On the shore and the stripes of the moon on the sand
Disappear and the sounds of the heron jerk
Across the lake, the growing blastula turns itself
Inside out unassisted and becomes a gut.

What is the source of the tension instigating next
The rudimentary tail and gills, the cobweb of veins?
What is the impetus slowly directing the hard-core
Current right up the scale to that one definite moment
When a fold of cells quivers suddenly for the first time

And someone says loudly "heart," born, beating steadily,
Bearing now in the white water of the moon
The instantaneous distinction of being liable to death?

Above me, the full moon, round and floating deep
In its capsule of sky, never trembles.
In ten thousand years it will never involute
Its white frozen blastula to form a gut,
Will never by a heart be called born.

Think of that part of me wishing tonight to remember
The split-second edge before the beginning,
To remember by a sudden white involution of sight,
By a vision of tension folding itself
Inside clear open waters, by imitating a manipulation
Of cells in a moment of distinction, wishing to remember
The entire language made during that crossing.

. . . . .

THE QUESTION OF AFFECTION

We don't know yet what it means to be touched,
To be the recipient of caresses, what the ear
Learns of itself when its lines are followed
By the finger of somebody else.

We know the spine of the infant can expand,
The neck grow sturdy, the shoulder blades facile
By fondling alone. The acuity of the eye is increased,
The lung capacity doubled by random nuzzles
To the ribs.

But we don't understand what the mind perceives
When the thigh's length is fixed by the dawdling

Of the lover's hand, when the girth of the waist
Is defined by the arms of a child.

An affectionate ear on the belly must alter
The conception of the earth pressing itself against the sky.
An elbow bent across the chest must anticipate
Early light angled over the lake. The curl of the pea
Can be understood as one hand caught carefully inside another.

Cores and cylinders, warm boundaries and disappearing curves,
What is it we realize when these interruptions of space
Are identified with love in the touch of somebody else?

I must remember now what it was I recognized
In the sky outside the window last night
As I felt the line of my shoulder drawn
In the trace of your lips.

. . . . .

SEDUCED BY EAR ALONE

Someone should explain how it happens, starting
With the dull stimulation of anvil and stirrups,
The established frequency of shifting air molecules
Initiated by your voice, entering my ear.
The mind, having learned how, can find the single silk
Strand of your breath anywhere, latch on and remember.

But not actually touching the body at all,
How do words alone ease the strictures of the palms,
Alter the tendency of the thighs, cause
The eyes to experience visions? I can see clearly
The stark white sliver of passion running a mile deep
In your whisper.

Maybe the ease of your voice suggests
The bliss of some previous state--sleeping
In a deep crevice at the top of a mountain, the eyes
Sealed tight, or being fed by motion in warm water
At the edge of the sea. By the twist of leaves
In a forest of poplars, I understand how light is fractioned
And born again in the aspects of your words.
I listen like an eddy in deep water turning easily
From one existence to another. I want now
To be covered by you.

And alone on any night, if the wind in the trees
Should sound by accident like the timbre of your voice,
I can be fooled for an instant, feeling suddenly in the dark
Estimable and saved.

. . . . .

ACHIEVING PERSPECTIVE

Straight up away from this road,
Away from the fitted particles of frost
Coating the hull of each chick pea,
And the stiff archer bug making its way
In the morning dark, toe hair by toe hair,
Up the stem of the trillium,
Straight up through the sky above this road right now,
The galaxies of the Cygnus A cluster
Are colliding with each other in a massive swarm
Of interpenetrating and exploding catastrophes.
I try to remember that.

And even in the gold and purple pretense
Of evening, I make myself remember
That it would take 40,000 years full of gathering

Into leaf and dropping, full of pulp splitting
And the hard wrinkling of seed, of the rising up
Of wood fibers and the disintegration of forests,
Of this lake disappearing completely in the bodies
Of toad slush and duckweed rock,
40,000 years and the fastest thing we own,
To reach the one star nearest to us.

And when you speak to me like this,
I try to remember that the wood and cement walls
Of this room are being swept away now,
Molecule by molecule, in a slow and steady wind,
And nothing at all separates our bodies
From the vast emptiness expanding, and I know
We are sitting in our chairs
Discoursing in the middle of the blackness of space.
And when you look at me
I try to recall that at this moment
Somewhere millions of miles beyond the dimness
Of the sun, the comet Biela, speeding
In its rocks and ices, is just beginning to enter
The widest arc of its elliptical turn.

. . . . .

THE MAN HIDDEN BEHIND THE DRAPES

When I entered the room and turned on the lights,
There were his feet bare beneath the edge
Of the draperies, his tendons flexed, the bony
Diamonds of his ankles shadowed. If I'd seen
His face I might have laughed.

Remember the naked feet of Christ seen so often,
Washed, kissed, dried in women's hair,

Or crossed and bleeding, pinioned
Like butterfly wings?

When I opened the door,
There were his feet below the drapes, as quiet
As if they lounged beneath a fine robe. Headlights
Moving slowly up the drive at this point
Would have fully exposed his nude body in the window,
His buttocks tensed, his face turned toward the glare
For that moment, then disappearing again into the darkness.

An artist might have pictured snow on the lawn
And a moon and a child looking out from the house
Across the way, watching the figure behind the glass,
The white panes across his back, his hands reaching
For the parting in the curtains.

When I entered the room the light spread first
In a rectangle straight across the floor to his feet,
His toes squeezing under in a crippled kind of gripping.
Someone watching from the end of the hall behind me
Would have seen my body framed in the light of the doorway
And beyond me the wall of the drapes.

Understand the particular axis at which he stood
In the vision of each different beholder, the multiple
Coordinates of hour and position and place coinciding
With the grids of light and sound and preceding
Interpretations. Consider that indeterminable effect
Of his being on the eye of the one unaware of his existence.

There is a house three blocks away that has no man
Behind the drapes. There is a house on a high sea wall
That has two men and no window. There is a house
That does not speak this language and consequently
Tells us nothing.

Almost laughing, my hand still on the door,
I stood watching his feet, and had there been an old woman
Living in the attic, then looking down through a chink in the ceiling
She would have seen in two dimensions, the knuckles of his toes,
The top of my head.

. . . . .

CONCEPTS AND THEIR BODIES
(THE BOY IN THE FIELD ALONE)

Staring at the mud turtle's eye
Long enough, he sees *concentricity* there
For the first time, as if it possessed
Pupil and iris and oracular lid,
As if it grew, forcing its own gene of circularity.
The concept is definitely
The cellular arrangement of sight.

The five amber grasses maintaining their seedheads
In the breeze against the sky
Have borne *latitude* from the beginning,
Secure *civility* like leaves in their folds.
He discovers *persistence* in the mouth
Of the caterpillar in the same way
As he discovers clear syrup
On the broken end of the dayflower,
Exactly as he comes accidentally upon
The mud crown of the crawfish.

The spotted length of the bullfrog leaping
Lakeward just before the footstep
Is not bullfrog, spread and sailing,
But the body of *initiative* with white glossy belly.
Departure is the wing let loose

By the dandelion, and it does possess
A sparse down and will not be thought of,
Even years later, even in the station
At midnight among the confusing lights,
As separate from that white twist
Of filament drifting.

Nothing is sharp enough to disengage
The butterfly's path from *erraticism*.

And *freedom* is this September field
Covered this far by tree shadows
Through which this child chooses to run
Until he chooses to stop,
And it will be so hereafter.

. . . . .

THE DETERMINATIONS OF
THE SCENE

Consider one born in the desert,
How he must see his sorrow rise
In the semblance of the yucca spreading
Its thorn-covered leaves in every direction,
Pricking clear to the ends
Of his fingers. He recognizes it
And deals with it thus. He learns to ponder
Like the reptile, in a posed quiet
Of the mind, to move on the barest
Essentials, to solve problems
Like the twisted mesquite sustaining itself.
He puts edges to the nouns of his statements,
Copying the distinct lines of the canyon in shadow,
And establishes cool niches out of the sun

In every part of his dogma. He understands
His ecstasy in terms of fluidity, high spring water
In motion through the arroyo.

That one born in the forest, growing up
With canopies, must seek to secure coverings
For all of his theories. He blesses trees
And boulders, the solid and barely altered.
He is biased in terms of stable growth vertically.
And doesn't he picture his thoughts springing
From moss and decay, from the white sponge
Of fungus and porous toadstools blending?
He is shaped by the fecund and the damp,
His fertile identifications with humus
And the aroma of rain on the deepening
Forest floor. Seeing the sky only in pieces
Of light, his widest definition must be modeled
After the clearing hemmed in by trees.

And consider the child raised near the sea, impinged
Upon constantly by the surf rising in swells,
Breaking itself to permanent particles of mist
Over the cliffs. Did you really think
The constant commotion of all that fury
Would mean nothing in the formation of the vocabulary
That he chooses to assign to God?
The surge, the explosion must constitute
The underlying dominion unacknowledged
In his approach to the cosmos.

And we mustn't forget to inquire:
Against what kinds of threats must the psyche
Of the Arctic child protect itself in sleep?

BEING OF THIS STATE

In the entire night sky, in all of the inverted
Slipped-back-upon-itself almost total emptiness
With its occasional faint clusters of pinprick
Fluctuations, there is not one single
Star grateful for its own light.

And on the stalk of blossoming confusion
Outside my door, barrelheads of camelia fistfuls,
There is not one petal that esteems
The ivory ellipse of its own outer edge
Or the molecules of its own scent escaping.

Who can detect a joy of beholding in the golden
Pipe fish filtering among the golden coral
Or in the blue-bred musk ox with its shaggy frost?
Which one among the tattered fungi remembers
The favor of the damp, the gift of decay?

Along the beach the Arctic terns rush forward
Up to their bellies in salt foam and shell-
Shag rolling, but not one is able to bless first
The mole crab it snips up and swallows.

Inside the network of the clearing, among the scritching
And skeetering, the thuz and the tremulous ching,
There is not one insect able to recognize the sound
Of its own beatification. Clinging to the weeds

In the middle of that broad field spread wide
And pressed against the open night, neither those insects,
Nor the hissing grasses, nor the ash-covered moon
Can ever contemplate the importance
Of the invention of praise.

SUPPOSITION

Suppose the molecular changes taking place
In the mind during the act of praise
Resulted in an emanation rising into space.
Suppose that emanation went forth
In the configuration of its occasion:
For instance, the design of rain pocks
On the lake's surface or the blue depths
Of the canyon with its horizontal cedars stunted.

Suppose praise had physical properties
And actually endured? What if the pattern
Of its disturbances rose beyond the atmosphere,
Becoming a permanent outline implanted in the cosmos--
The sound of the celebratory banjo or horn
Lodging near the third star of Orion's belt;
Or to the east of the Pleiades, an atomic
Disarrangement of the words,
"How particular, the pod-eyed hermit crab
And his prickly orange legs"?

Suppose benevolent praise,
Coming into being by our will,
Had a separate existence, its purple or azure light
Gathering in the upper reaches, affecting
The aura of morning haze over autumn fields,
Or causing a perturbation in the mode of an asteroid.
What if praise and its emanations
Were necessary catalysts to the harmonious
Expansion of the void? Suppose, for the prosperous
Welfare of the universe, there were an element
Of need involved.

A GIANT HAS SWALLOWED THE EARTH

What will it do for him, to have internalized
The many slender stems of riverlets and funnels,
The blunt toes of the pinecone fallen, to have ingested
Lakes in gold slabs at dawn and the peaked branches
Of the fir under snow? He has taken into himself
The mist of the hazel nut, the white hairs of the moth,
And the mole's velvet snout. He remembers, by inner
Voice alone, fogs over frozen grey marshes, fine
Salt on the blunt of the cliff.

What will it mean to him to perceive things
First from within--the mushroom's fold, the martin's
Tongue, the spotted orange of the wallaby's ear,
To become the object himself before he comprehends it,
Putting into perfect concept without experience
The din of the green gully in spring mosses?

And when he stretches on his bed and closes his eyes,
What patterns will appear to him naturally--the schematic
Tracings of the Vanessa butterfly in migration, tacks
And red strings marking the path of each mouse
In the field, nucleic chromosomes aligning their cylinders
In purple before their separation? The wind must settle
All that it carries behind his face and rise again
In his vision like morning.

A giant has swallowed the earth,
And when he sleeps now, o when he sleeps,
How his eyelids murmur, how we envy his dream.

THE SIGNIFICANCE OF LOCATION

The cat has the chance to make the sunlight
Beautiful, to stop it and turn it immediately
Into black fur and motion, to take it
As shifting branch and brown feather
Into the back of the brain forever.

The cardinal has flown the sun in red
Through the oak forest to the lawn.
The finch has caught it in yellow
And taken it among the thorns. By the spider
It has been bound tightly and tied
In an eight-stringed knot.

The sun has been intercepted in its one
Basic state and changed to a million varieties
Of green stick and tassel. It has been broken
Into pieces by glass rings, by mist
Over the river. Its heat
Has been given the board fence for body,
The desert rock for fact. On winter hills
It has been laid down in white like a martyr.

This afternoon we could spread gold scarves
Clear across the field and say in truth,
"Sun you are silk."

Imagine the sun totally isolated,
Its brightness shot in continuous streaks straight out
Into the black, never arrested,
Never once being made light.

Someone should take note
Of how the earth has saved the sun from oblivion.

MAKING A HISTORY

The glutinous snail
In silvery motion
Has rubbed his neck
Against his mate's, covered
Her side-slatted orifice
With his own. The newt,
Jumping suddenly forward underwater,
Has twisted and dropped
His pocket of sperm. And in the field
The fritillary, frenzied for orange,
Has skittered straight up and hovered.

The chortle of the Siamese fighting fish
Held upside down by her mate
Has subsided. The dragon fish
Has chewed the tail of his lover,
And the frigate has been swollen
Three times, burgeoning in red.
Bison have risen from their dirt clouds
Blowing. Antlers have entangled, caribou
Collided, cockerels have caught hold,
And the crack of the mountain sheep meeting
Has broken over the arroyo, and the bowerbirds
Have howled and the fruit bats screamed,
And the wild pigs have lain down
In punctuated barking, and the zigzag cocking
Of the stickleback has widened, and alligators
Have spit and strumped, thrashing
In the crumpled reeds. Storks have bent backward
Rooting at heaven with their long beaks banging,
And the alley cat, in guttural moaning,
Has finally been released, bleeding
At the neck, and everyone
Has something to remember.

ON THE EXISTENCE OF THE SOUL

How confident I am it is there. Don't I bring it,
As if it were enclosed in a fine leather case,
To particular places solely for its own sake?
Haven't I set it down before the variegated canyon
And the undeviating bald salt dome?
Don't I feed it on ivory calcium and ruffled
Shell bellies, shore boulders, on the sight
Of the petrel motionless over the sea, its splayed
Feet hanging? Don't I make sure it apprehends
The invisibly fine spray more than once?

I have seen that it takes in every detail
I can manage concerning the garden wall and its borders.
I have listed for it the comings and goings
Of one hundred species of insects explicitly described.
I have named the chartreuse stripe
And the fimbriated antenna, the bulbed thorax
And the multiple eye. I have sketched
The brilliant wings of the trumpet vine and invented
New vocabularies describing the interchanges between rocks
And their crevices, between the holly lip
And its concept of itself.

And if not for its sake, why would I go
Out into the night alone and stare deliberately
Straight up into 15 billion years ago and more?

I have cherished it. I have named it.
By my own solicitations
I have proof of its presence.

ALL THE ELEMENTS OF THE SCENE

In the upper right-hand corner of this scene is a copse
Of cottonwood *(Populus deltoides)*. Each leaf
Like a silver dollar twists on its flattened stalk.
And parallel to the edge of this scene runs
A line of forest, thin dwarf oak, scrub vine,
The smoketree. Leaning to the left of that, a field
Of flat grasses sways, heavy with thorny seeds. Blue
Toadflax and bee balm bend in the wind toward
The bare rim of the pond in the foreground, its lazy
Wash surfaced with baweedle bug, the raised eyes
Of the leopard frog *(Rana pipiens)*. Pickerelweeds
Make hostage of the dragonfly, the nesting mud tortoise.

Here am I in this scene too, my shadow wrinkling
On the water of the pond, my footprints making pools
Along the bank. And all that I say, each word
That I give to this scene is part of the scene. The act
Of each thing identified being linked to its name
Becomes an object itself here. The bumblebee hovers
Near the bitter orange of the mallow weed. That sentence
And this one too are elements of the scene.

This poem, as real as the carp sliding in green
At the bottom of the pond, is the only object
Within the scene capable of discussing both itself
And the scene. The moist, rotting log sinks
Into earth. The pink toothwort sprouts beside it.
The poem of this scene has 34 lines.

And see, reader, you are here also, watching
As the poem speaks to you, as it points out that you
Were present at the very first word. The fact of your
Cognizance here is established as you read this sentence.

23

Take note of the existence of the words in this scene
As they tell you--the pond is purple; the sun is blocked
In branches below the oak; there are shadows
On this poem; night things are stirring.

.   .   .   .   .

THAT SONG

I will use the cormorant on his rope at night diving
Into the sea, and the fire on the prow, and the fish
Like ribbons sliding toward the green light in the dark.

I will remember the baneberry and the bladderwort
And keep the white crone under the bosackle tree
And the translucent figs and the candelabra burning alone
In the middle of the plains, and the twig girdler,
And the lizard of Christ running over the waves.

I will take the egg bubble on the flute
Of the elm and the ministries of the predacious
Caul beetle, the spit of the iris, the red juice shot
From the eye of the horny toad, and I will use
The irreducible knot wound by the hazel scrub
And the bog myrtle still tangling, and the sea horse
With his delicate horn, the flywheel of his maneuvering.

I will remember exactly each tab folded down
In the sin book of Sister Alleece and each prayer
Hanging in its painted cylinder above the door
And the desert goat at noon facing
The sun to survive.

I will include the brindled bandicoot and the barnacle
Goose and the new birds hatching from mussels

Under the sea and the migrating wildebeests humming
Like organs, moaning like men.

The sand swimmers alive under the Gobi plateau,
The cactus wren in her nest of thorns and the herald
Of the tarantula wasp and each yellow needle
In the spring field rising, everything will be there,
And nothing will be wasted.

.   .   .   .   .

THE FEAR OF FALLING

It comes from the tree apes, this instinct
To grasp, to fill the hollow of the hand
And fasten. Emerging from the womb,
How each must have clawed, grabbing before breathing,
Its mother's hairy knee, the slip of her rump.
Imagine the weak, the unimpressed, dropping
Through leaves like stones to the ground below.

The mind has become itself inside the panic
Of bodies falling with fingers spread useless.
How many times in the jerk of sleep
Has the last hand-hold been seen
Disappearing upward like a small bird sucked into space?

Bound to the clenching habit of the fingers, united
With the compulsion of the hands to grasp, the mind
Perceives in terms of possession, recognizing
Its lack from the beginning--the black fur
Of the void, the bowl of the wide belly, the dark
Of that great invented thigh out of reach.

The first need of the brain is to curl
The conceptual knuckles and tighten.
And whether it is on each warm-water crack
At the bottom of the sea or on every maneuver
Of the swamp muskrat or around the grey spiral
Details of forgiveness, the grip of the brain
Is determined not to be negligible.

Here in the wind at the top of these branches
We recognize
The persistent need to take hold of something
Known to be sure-footed.

. . . .

CAPTURING THE SCENE

With pen and ink, the artist takes care
To be explicit, each board of the covered bridge
Elucidated, each shingle of the roof. The columns
Of the termites and the holes of the borers to be,
He remembers. He is deliberate to denote those specifics
He understands, filling in the blank with the pause
Of the dragonfly, the scratch of the myrtle weed.
He watches to maintain in his lines exactly
That tedious balance between the river in motion
And the river itself. Like wires, he coordinates
The trees and their affinity for disorder.

How skillfully he locates the woodthrush clearing
The last field beyond the hills, and the worn rocks
Along the bank, each with its own specific hump
Against space. He acknowledges the sunken
And the sucked away, the shadows on the far left
Bearing witness to objects still outside the scene.

And notice how he achieves that incandescence of ink
Around the seed pod. He knows that the scream of the jay,
The odor of the sun-dried wood is entirely in his stroke.
Without making a single mark, he executes the heavens.

And hasn't he understood from the beginning where he must never
Look directly--into the dark hedgerow on the opposite bank,
Among the crossed sticks of the rushes and the spaces between,
How he must not stare steadily at the long fall
Of the sky below the horizon or probe too deeply that area
Lying between the ink and its line on the paper? He knows
There is that which he must draw blindfolded or not at all.
And before he can give to the scene its final name,
He must first identify every facet of its multiplicity
In detail; he must then turn away his face completely
And remember more.

THE TATTOOED LADY IN
THE GARDEN (1986)

THE PIECES OF HEAVEN

No one alone could detail that falling--the immediate
Sharpening and blunting of particle and plane,
The loosening, the congealing of axis
And field, the simultaneous opening and closing
Composing the first hardening of moment when heaven first broke
From wholeness into infinity.

No one alone could follow the falling
Of all those pieces gusting in tattered
Layers of mirage like night rain over a rocky hill,
Pieces cartwheeling like the red-banded leg
Of the locust, rolling like elk antlers dropping
After winter, spiraling slowly like a fossil of squid
Twisting to the bottom of the sea, pieces lying toppled
Like bison knees on a prairie, like trees of fern
In a primeval forest.

And no one could remember the rising
Of all those pieces in that moment, pieces shining
Like cottonwood dust floating wing-side up
Across the bottomland, rising like a woman easily
Lifting to meet her love, like the breasting,
The disappearing surge and scattering crest of fire

Or sea blown against rock, bannered like the quills
Of lionfish in their sway, like the whippling stripe
Of the canebrake rattler under leaves.

Who can envision all of heaven trembling
With the everlasting motion of its own shattering
Into the piece called honor and the piece
Called terror and the piece called death and the piece
Tracing the piece called compassion all the way back
To its source in that initial crimp of potential particle
Becoming the inside and outside called matter and space?

And no one alone can describe entirely
This single piece of heaven partially naming its own falling
Or the guesswork forming the piece
That is heaven's original breaking, the imagined
Piece that is its new and eventual union.

.   .   .   .   .

SECOND WITNESS

The only function of the red-cupped fruit
Hanging from the red stem of the sassafras
Is to reveal the same shiny blue orb of berry
Existing in me.

The only purpose of the row of hemlocks blowing
On the rocky ridge is to give form to the crossed lines
And clicking twigs, the needle-leaf matrix
Of evergreen motion I have always possessed.

Vega and the ring nebula and the dust
Of the Pleiades have made clear by themselves
The constellations inherent to my eyes.

What is it I don't know of myself
From never having seen a crimson chat at its feeding
Or the dunnart carrying its young? It must be imperative
That I watch the entire hardening of the bud
Of the clove, that I witness the flying fish breaking
Into sky through the sun-smooth surface of the sea.

I ask the winter wren nesting in the clogged roots
Of the fallen oak to remember the multitoned song
Of itself in my ears, and I ask the short-snouted
Silver twig weevil to be particular and the fishhook
Cactus to be tenacious. I thank the distinct edges
Of the six-spined spider crab for their peculiarities
And praise the freshwater eel for its graces. I urge
The final entanglement of blade and light to keep
Its secrecy, and I beg the white-tailed kite this afternoon,
For my sake, to be keen-eyed, to soar well, to be quick
To make me known.

.   .   .   .   .

HER DELIGHT
After Psalms 1:2, 3

The tupelo, the blackgum and the poplar,
The overcup oak and the water hickory stand
Along the riverbank being eternal law all day.
They have risen, transforming soil, yielding
To each other, spreading and bending in easy-sun
Contortions, just as their branches decreed they must
During their rising.

Their shadows cast shadow-law this evening
In the long narrow bars of steady black they make
Over the river, being the permanent mathematical
Matrixes they invent relative to the height
Of their ascending trunks.

And the law taking in the soft moisture
Of slow, pervading rivers underground
Is called root. And the root consistently sorting
Ion and mineral by the describable properties
Of its gated skin is called law.

The plum-shaped fruit of the tupelo
Is the rule defining the conformity
To which it shapes itself. The orange berry
Of the possumhaw creates the sugary orange law
Of the sun by which it makes its reality.
Every flattened pit and dark blue drupe and paper-skin
Seed obeys perfectly the commandment it fashions
By becoming itself.

The trees only write the eternal law
Of whatever they have written—the accomplishment
Of the blackgum ordaining autumn red
In the simultaneous commandment of its scarlet leaves;
The accomplishment of the hickory branching
Its leaf in naked, thin-veined everlasting statutes
Of yellow across the sky.

And the woman standing this evening beneath the river trees,
Watching them rise by fissured bark, by husked and hardened
Fruit held high above the water, watching the long bodies
Of their shadows lying unmoved across the current,
She is the easy law that states she must become,
In the hazy, leaf-encroached columns of the evening sun,
Her meditation in this delight.

It always happens, looking up to the tops
Of the sycamores still white and yellow with sunlight
Above the dark river bottom, or bending back to see
The wind, heard first as a caravan of paper horses
In the upper branches of the pines, or following
The flurried lightning bug to where it disappears
Above the parsley haw then catches on again
Even higher, raising the eyes that high,
The body begins to feel again something of significance.

Maybe it's the result of some predisposition
We've inherited from the trees, something in the genes
Promoting a belief in the importance of ascension
Or reaffirming the 70-million-year-old conviction
That stretching one leaf higher might be enough
To finally discover the sky. There's a feeling
In the body of a conviction like that.

Maybe the act of tilting the head backward
To search the sky for Mizar or Draco
Merely flexes the spinal cord at the neck,
Thus doubling the strength of every impulse
Passing there, or maybe sight is actually deepened
When blood flows backward from the eyes,
Or maybe more oxygen, helped by gravity
To the frontal lobe, expands the normal boundaries
Of the perceived heavens.

It might be something as simple as that.
But it's certain, watching the pale-pearl angle
Of the early evening moon, or following the five
Black cowbirds reel across the greying clouds,
Or tracing the easy drift of a cottonwood seed

Slowly rising directly overhead, it's certain,
There's bound to be something new again of power
Astir in the body.

.   .   .   .   .

LOVE SONG

It's all right, together with me tonight,
How your whole body trembles exactly like the locust
Establishing its dry-cymbal quivering
Even in the farthest branch-tip leaves
Of the tree in which it screams.

Lying next to me, it's all right how similar
You become to the red deer in its agitated pacing
On the open plains by the sea, in its sidling
Haunch against haunch, in the final mastery
Of its mounting.

And it's all right, in those moments,
How you possess the same single-minded madness
Of the opened wood poppy circling and circling,
The same wild strength of its golden eye.

It's true. You're no better
Than the determined boar snorgling and rooting,
No better than the ridiculous, ruffled drumming
Of the prairie chicken, no better
Than the explosion of the milkweed pod
Spilling the white furl of the moon deep
In the midnight field. You're completely
Indistinguishable from the enraged sand myrtle
Absurd in its scarlet spread on the rocky bluffs.

But it's all right. Don't you know
This is precisely what I seek, mad myself
To envelope every last drupe and pearl-dropped ovule,
Every nip and cry and needle-fine boring, every drooping,
Spore-rich tassel of oak flower, all the whistling,
Wing-beating, heavy-tipped matings of an entire prairie
Of grasses, every wafted, moaning seed hook
You can possibly manage to bring to me,
That this is exactly what I contrive to take into my arms
With you, again and again.

. . . . .

THE HUMMINGBIRD: A SEDUCTION

If I were a female hummingbird perched still
And quiet on an upper myrtle branch
In the spring afternoon and if you were a male
Alone in the whole heavens before me, having parted
Yourself, for me, from cedar top and honeysuckle stem
And earth down, your body hovering in midair
Far away from jewelweed, thistle and bee balm;

And if I watched how you fell, plummeting before me,
And how you rose again and fell, with such mastery
That I believed for a moment *you* were the sky
And the red-marked bird diving inside your circumference
Was just the physical revelation of the light's
Most perfect desire;

And if I saw your sweeping and sucking
Performance of swirling egg and semen in the air,
The weaving, twisting vision of red petal
And nectar and soaring rump, the rush of your wing
In its grand confusion of arcing and splitting
Created completely out of nothing just for me,

Then when you came down to me, I would call you
My own spinning bloom of ruby sage, my funneling
Storm of sunlit sperm and pollen, my only breathless
Piece of scarlet sky, and I would bless the base
Of each of your feathers and touch the tine
Of string muscles binding your wings and taste
The odor of your glistening oils and hunt
The honey in your crimson flare
And I would take you and take you and take you
Deep into any kind of nest you ever wanted.

.   .   .   .   .

THE POWER OF TOADS

The oak toad and the red-spotted toad love their love
In a spring rain, calling and calling, breeding
Through a stormy evening clasped atop their mates.
Who wouldn't sing—anticipating the belly pressed hard
Against a female's spine in the steady rain
Below writhing skies, the safe moist jelly effluence
Of a final exaltation?

There might be some toads who actually believe
That the loin-shaking thunder of the banks, the evening
Filled with damp, the warm softening mud and rising
Riverlets are the facts of their own persistent
Performance. Maybe they think that when they sing
They sing more than songs, creating rain and mist
By their voices, initiating the union of water and dusk,
Females materializing on the banks shaped perfectly
By their calls.

And some toads may be convinced they have forced
The heavens to twist and moan by the continual expansion
Of their lung sacs pushing against the dusk.

And some might believe the splitting light,
The soaring grey they see above them are nothing
But a vision of the longing in their groins,
A fertile spring heaven caught in its entirety
At the pit of the gut.

And they might be right.
Who knows whether these broken heavens
Could exist tonight separate from trills and toad ringings?
Maybe the particles of this rain descending on the pond
Are nothing but the visual manifestation of whistles
And cascading love clicks in the shore grasses.
Raindrops-finding-earth and coitus could very well
Be known here as one.

We could investigate the causal relationship
Between rainstorm and love-by-pondside if we wished.
We could lie down in the grasses by the water's edge
And watch to see exactly how the heavens were moved,
Thinking hard of thunder, imagining all the courses
That slow, clean waters might take across our bodies,
Believing completely in the rolling and pressing power
Of heavens and thighs. And in the end we might be glad,
Even if all we discovered for certain was the slick, sweet
Promise of good love beneath dark skies inside warm rains.

.   .   .   .   .

THE POSSIBLE SALVATION OF
CONTINUOUS MOTION

Adapted from a love letter written by E. Lotter (1872–1930)

If we could be taken alone together in a driverless
Sleigh pulled by horses with blinders over endless
Uninhabited acres of snow; if the particles
Of our transgression could be left behind us

Scattered across the woodlands and frozen lakes
Like pieces of light scattered over the flashing snow;

If the initiation and accomplishment of our act
In that sleigh could be separated by miles
Of forest--the careful parting begun
Under the ice-covered cedars, the widening and entering
Accomplished in swirls of frost racing along the hills,
The removal and revelation coming beside the seesaw shifting
Of grassheads rustling in the snowy ditches; all the elements
Of our interaction left in a thousand different places--
Thigh against thigh with the drowsy owlets in the trees
Overhead, your face caught for an instant above mine
In one eye of the snow hare;

If the horses could go fast enough across the ice
So that no one would ever be able to say, "Sin
Was committed *here,*" our sin being as diffuse
As broken bells sounding in molecules of ringing
Clear across the countryside;

And under the blanket beside you in the sleigh,
If I could watch the night above the flying heads
Of the horses, if I could see our love exploded
Like stars cast in a black sky over the glassy plains
So that nothing, not even the mind of an angel,
Could ever reassemble that deed;

Well, I would go with you right now,
Dearest, immediately, while the horses
Are still biting and strapping in their reins.

THE DELIGHT OF BEING LOST

There are times when one might wish to be nothing
But the plain crease and budded nipple
Of a breast, nothing but the manner in the lay
Of an arm across a pillow or the pressure of hips
And shoulders on a sheet. Sometimes there is a desire
To draw down into the dull turn of the inner knee, dumb
And isolated from the cognizant details of any summer night,
To be chin and crotch solely as the unrecorded, passing
Moments of themselves, to have no name or place but breath.

If wished enough, it might be possible to sink away completely,
To leave the persistent presence of pine trees
Brushing against the eaves, loons circling the lake,
Making an issue of direction; to sink away, remaining
Awake inside the oblivion deep within a naked thigh,
To open the eyes inside the blindness of a wrist, hearing
Nothing but the deafness in the curve of the neck.

It would seem a perfect joy to me tonight
To lie still in this darkness, to deny everything
But the rise in the line of ankle or spine, ignoring
The angles of walls establishing definable spaces,
Ignoring the clear, moon-shadow signals of specific
Circumstance, to recognize no reality but the universal
Anonymity of a particular body which might then be stroked
And kissed and fondled and worshipped without ever knowing
Or caring to ask by whom or where or how it was given
Such pleasure.

THE DEFINITION OF TIME

In the same moment
That Kioka's great-great-grandfather died,
11,000 particles of frost dissolved into dew
On the blades of the woodrush,
And three water lily leaf beetles paused
Anticipating light making movements
Of their bodies in the weeds.

And in that same moment an earthworm
Swallowed a single red spore down its slimmest
Vein, and the chimney crayfish shoveled a whisker farther
Through slick pond-bottom silt, and one slow
Slice of aster separated its purple segment
From the bud.

Simultaneously the mossy granite along the ridge shifted
Two grains on its five-mile fault, and the hooves
Of ewe and pony, damp in the low-field fog,
Shook with that shift. The early hawk on the post
Blinked a drop of mist from its eye, and the black tern
With a cry flew straight up, remembering the marsh
By scent alone over the sandy hills.

And in that instant the field, carried
Without consent through the dark, held
Its sedges steady for the first turn
Into the full orange sun, and each tense sliver
Of pine on the mountains far to the east
Shone hot already in a white noon,
And in the dark night-sea far behind the field and forest,
The head of a single shark sperm pierced
An ovum and became blood.

The twelfth ring of the tallest redwood
Hardened its circle, and the first lick of the hatching
Goatweed butterfly was made tongue. And Kioka
And his ancestors call the infinite and continuous
Record they make of this moment, "The Book
Of the Beginning and the Chronicle of the End."

. . . . .

THE POSSIBLE SUFFERING OF A
GOD DURING CREATION

It might be continuous--the despair he experiences
Over the imperfection of the unfinished, the weaving
Body of the imprisoned moonfish, for instance,
Whose invisible arms in the mid-waters of the deep sea
Are not yet free, or the velvet-blue vervain
Whose grainy tongue will not move to speak, or the ear
Of the spitting spider still oblivious to sound.

It might be pervasive--the anguish he feels
Over the falling away of everything that the duration
Of the creation must, of necessity, demand, maybe feeling
The break of each and every russet-headed grass
Collapsing under winter ice or feeling the split
Of each dried and brittle yellow wing of the sycamore
As it falls from the branch. Maybe he winces
At each particle-by-particle disintegration of the limestone
Ledge into the crevasse and the resulting compulsion
Of the crevasse to rise grain by grain, obliterating itself.

And maybe he suffers from the suffering
Inherent to the transitory, feeling grief himself
For the grief of shattered beaches, disembodied bones
And claws, twisted squid, piles of ripped and tangled,

Uprooted turtles and rock crabs and Jonah crabs,
Sand bugs, seaweed and kelp.

How can he stand to comprehend the hard, pitiful
Unrelenting cycles of coitus, ovipositors, sperm and zygotes,
The repeated unions and dissolutions over and over,
The constant tenacious burying and covering and hiding
And nesting, the furious nurturing of eggs, the bright
Breaking-forth and the inevitable cold blowing-away?

Think of the million million dried stems of decaying
Dragonflies, the thousand thousand leathery cavities
Of old toads, the mounds of cows' teeth, the tufts
Of torn fur, the contorted eyes, the broken feet, the rank
Bloated odors, the fecund brown-haired mildews
That are the residue of his process. How can he tolerate knowing
There is nothing else here on earth as bright and salty
As blood spilled in the open?

Maybe he wakes periodically at night,
Wiping away the tears he doesn't know
He has cried in his sleep, not having had time yet to tell
Himself precisely how it is he must mourn, not having had time yet
To elicit from his creation its invention
Of his own solace.

. . . . .

THE VERIFICATION OF
VULNERABILITY: BOG TURTLE

Guarded by horned beak and nails, surrounded
By mahogany carapace molded in tiles
Like beveled wood, hidden within the hingeless
Plastron, beneath twelve, yellow-splotched

Black scutes, buried below the inner lungs
And breast, harbored in the far reaches
Of the living heart, there it exists,
As it must, that particle of vulnerability,
As definite in its place as if it were a brief glint
Of steel, buried inside the body of the bog turtle.

And it is carried in that body daily, like a pinpoint
Of diamond in a dark pouch, through marshy fields
And sunlit seepages, and it is borne in that body,
Like a crystal of salt-light locked in a case
Of night, borne through snail-ridden reeds and pungent
Cow pastures in spring. It is cushioned and bound
By folds of velvet, by flesh and the muscle
Of dreams, during sleep on a weedy tussock all afternoon.
It is divided and bequeathed again in June, protected
By thick sap, by yolk meal and forage inside its egg
Encompassed by the walls of shell and nest.

Maybe I can imagine the sole intention present
In the steady movement of turtle breath filled
With the odor of worms this morning, stirring
Clover moisture at the roots. Maybe I can understand
How the body has taken form solely
Around the possibility of its own death,
How the entire body of the bog turtle
Cherishes and maintains and verifies the existence
Of its own crucial point of vulnerability exactly
As if that point were the only distinct,
Dimensionless instant of eternity ever realized.
And maybe I can guess what it is we own,
If, in fact, it is true: the proof of possession
Is the possibility of loss.

JUSTIFICATION OF
THE HORNED LIZARD

I don't know why the horned lizard wants to live.
It's so ugly—short prickly horns and scowling
Eyes, lipless smile forced forever by bone,
Hideous scaly hollow where its nose should be.

I don't know what the horned lizard has to live for,
Skittering over the sun-irritated sand, scraping
The hot dusty brambles. It never sees anything but gravel
And grit, thorns and stickery insects, the towering
Creosote bush, the ocotillo and its whiplike
Branches, the severe edges of the Spanish dagger.
Even shade is either barren rock or barb.

The horned lizard will never know
A lush thing in its life. It will never see the flower
Of the water-filled lobelia bent over a clear
Shallow creek. It will never know moss floating
In waves in the current by the bank or the blue-blown
Fronds of the water clover. It will never have a smooth
Glistening belly of white like the bullfrog or a dew-heavy
Trill like the mating toad. It will never slip easily
Through mud like the skink or squat in the dank humus
At the bottom of a decaying forest in daytime.
It will never be free of dust. The only drink it will ever know
Is in the body of a bug.

And the horned lizard possesses nothing noble—
Embarrassing tail, warty hide covered with sharp dirty
Scales. No touch to its body, even from its own kind,
Could ever be delicate or caressing.

I don't know why the horned lizard wants to live.
Yet threatened, it burrows frantically into the sand
With a surprisingly determined fury of forehead, limbs
And ribs. Pursued, it even fights for itself, almost rising up,
Posturing on its bowed legs, propelling blood out of its eyes
In tight straight streams shot directly at the source
Of its possible extinction. It fights for itself,
Almost rising up, as if the performance of that act,
The posture, the propulsion of the blood itself,
Were justification enough and the only reason needed.

.   .   .   .   .

EULOGY FOR A HERMIT CRAB

You were consistently brave
On these surf-drenched rocks, in and out of their salty
Slough holes around which the entire expanse
Of the glinting grey sea and the single spotlight
Of the sun went spinning and spinning and spinning
In a tangle of blinding spume and spray
And pistol-shot collisions your whole life long.
You stayed. Even with the wet icy wind of the moon
Circling your silver case night after night after night
You were here.

And by the gritty orange curve of your claws,
By the soft, wormlike grip
Of your hinter body, by the unrelieved wonder
Of your black-pea eyes, by the mystified swing
And swing and swing of your touching antennae,
You maintained your name meticulously, you kept
Your name intact exactly, day after day after day.
No one could say you were less than perfect
In the hermitage of your crabness.

Now, beside the racing, incomprehensible racket
Of the sea stretching its great girth forever
Back and forth between this direction and another,
Please let the words of this proper praise I speak
Become the identical and proper sound
Of my mourning.

.   .   .   .   .

TRINITY

I wish something slow and gentle and good
Would happen to me, a patient and prolonged
Kind of happiness coming in the same way evening
Comes to a wide-branched sycamore standing
In an empty field; each branch, not succumbing,
Not taken, but feeling its entire existence
A willing revolution of cells; even asleep,
Feeling a decision of gold spreading
Over its ragged bark and motionless knots of seed,
Over every naked, vulnerable juncture; each leaf
Becoming a lavender shell, a stem-deep line
Of violet turning slowly and carefully to possess exactly
The pale and patient color of the sky coming.

I wish something that slow and that patient
Would come to me, maybe like the happiness
Growing when the lover's hand, easy on the thigh
Or easy on the breast, moves like late light moves
Over the branches of a sycamore, causing
A slow revolution of decision in the body;
Even asleep, feeling the spread of hazy coral
And ivory-grey rising through the legs and spine
To alter the belief behind the eyes; feeling the slow
Turn of wave after wave of acquiescence moving

From the inner throat to the radiance of a gold belly
To a bone center of purple; an easy, slow-turning
Happiness of possession like that, prolonged.

I wish something that gentle and that careful
And that patient would come to me. Death
Might be that way if one knew how to wait for it,
If death came easily and slowly,
If death were good.

. . . . .

THE CREATION OF THE INAUDIBLE

Maybe no one can distinguish which voice
Is god's voice sounding in a summer dusk
Because he calls with the same rising frequency,
The same rasp and rattling rustle the cicadas use
As they cling to the high leaves in the glowing
Dust of the oaks.

His exclamations might blend so precisely with the final
Crises of the swallows settling before dark
That no one will ever be able to say with certainty,
"That last long cry winging over the rooftop
Came from god."

Breathy and low, the vibrations of his nightly
Incantations could easily be masked by the scarcely
Audible hush of the lakeline dealing with the rocky shore,
And when a thousand dry sheaths of rushes and thistles
Stiffen and shiver in an autumn wind, anyone can imagine
How quickly and irretrievably his whisper might be lost.

Someone far away must be saying right now:
The only unique sound of his being
Is the spoken postulation of his unheard presence.

For even if he found the perfect chant this morning
And even if he played the perfect strings to accompany it,
Still, no one could be expected to know,
Because the blind click beetle flipping in midair,
And the slider turtle easing through the black iris bog,
And two savannah pines shedding dawn in staccato pieces
Of falling sun are already engaged in performing
The very same arrangement themselves.

.   .   .   .   .

PARLOR GAME ON A SNOWY
WINTER NIGHT

Albert, standing at the window, began by saying,
"False china eggs in a chicken's nest stimulate
The hen to lay eggs that are real,
And they also occasionally fool weasels."

"Telling the truth to a chicken then,"
Replied Sonia, "must be considered a grievous sin,
And deception, in this case, an extraordinary virtue."

"Chickens, brooding on china eggs as well as real ones,"
Said Cecil, rubbing his chin, "might regard glass eggs
As admirably false, but a weasel nosing the nest
Would consider glass eggs a malevolent tomfoolery
And the devil's own droppings."

"A weasel, testing the reality of eggs,
Must find glass and albumen
Equally easy to identify," continued Albert.

"China eggs, whether warm or not," said Felicia,
Mocking herself in the mirror, "at least consistently maintain
Their existence as false eggs."

"Perhaps the true egg, unable to maintain its reality
For long, is actually a weak imitation
Of the eternal nature of the glass egg," said Albert,
Drawing his initials on the frosty windowpane.

"Someone must investigate how the real image
Of a false egg in the chicken's true eye causes the cells
Of a potential egg to become an actuality," said Gordon,
Laying his book on the table.

"Can we agree then that the false china egg,
A deceptive but actual instigator,
Is the first true beginning of the chicken yard?"
Asked Sonia, filling in the last line of the game sheet.

Albert, rushing outdoors to discover
What the dogs had cornered in the brush beside the barn,
Found a weasel in the snow
With bloody yolk on its whiskers and a broken tooth.

. . . . .

FINDING THE TATTOOED LADY
IN THE GARDEN

Circus runaway, tattooed from head to toe in yellow
Petals and grape buds, rigid bark and dust-streaked
Patterns of summer, she lives naked among the hedges

50

And bordered paths of the garden. She hardly
Has boundaries there, so definite is her place.

Sometimes the golden flesh of the butterfly,
Quiet and needled in the spot of sun on her shoulder,
Can be seen and sometimes the wide blue wing
Of her raised hand before the maple and sometimes
The crisscrossed thicket, honeysuckle and fireweed,
Of her face. As she poses perfectly, her legs apart,
Some people can find the gentian-smooth meadow-skin showing
Through the distant hickory groves painted up her thighs
And the warm white windows of open sky appearing
Among the rose blossoms and vines of her breasts.

Shadow upon tattooed shadow upon real shadow,
She is there in the petaled skin of the iris
And the actual violet scents overlapping
At the bend of her arm, beneath and beyond
The initial act announcing the stems
Of the afternoon leafed and spread
In spires of green along her ribs, the bronze
Lizard basking at her navel.

Some call her searched-for presence the being
Of being, the essential garden of the garden.
And some call the continuing postulation
Of her location the only underlying structure,
The single form of flux, the final proof
And presence of crafted synonymy.
And whether the shadows of the sweetgum branches
Above her shift in the breeze across her breasts
Or whether she herself sways slightly
Beneath the still star-shaped leaves of the quiet
Forest overhead or whether the sweetgum shadows
Tattooed on her torso swell and linger
As the branches above are stirred by her breath,

The images possessed by the seekers are one
And the same when they know them as such.

And in the dark of late evening,
Isn't it beautiful the way they watch for her
To turn slowly, displaying the constellations
Penned in light among the black leaves
And blossoms of her back, the North Star
In its only coordinates shining at the base
Of her neck, the way they study the first glowing
Rim of the moon rising by its own shape
From the silvered curve of her brilliant hip?

.   .   .   .   .

DISCOVERING YOUR SUBJECT

Painting a picture of the same shrimp boat
Every day of your life might not be so boring.
For a while you could paint only in the mornings,
Each one different, the boat gold in the new sun
On your left, or the boat in predawn fog condensing
Mist. You might have to wait years, rising early
Over and over, to catch that one winter morning when frost
Becomes a boat. You could attempt to capture
The fragile potential inherent in that event.

You might want to depict the easy half-circle
Movements of the boat's shadows crossing over themselves
Through the day. You could examine every line
At every moment—the tangle of nets caught
In the orange turning of evening, the drape of the ropes
Over the rising moon.

You could spend considerable time just concentrating
On boat and birds—Boat with Birds Perched on Bow,

Boat with Birds Overhead, Shadows of Birds Covering
Hull and Deck, or Boat the Size of a Bird,
Bird in the Heart of the Boat, Boat with Wings,
Boat in Flight. Any endeavor pursued long enough
Assumes a momentum and direction all its own.

Or you might decide to lie down one day behind a clump
Of marsh rosemary on the beach, to see the boat embedded
In the blades of the saltwort or show how strangely
The stalk of the clotbur can rise higher than the mast.
Boat Caught like a Flower in the Crotch of the Sand Verbena.

After picturing the boat among stars, after discovering
The boat as revealed by rain, you might try painting
The boat in the eye of the gull or the boat in the eye
Of the sun or the boat in the eye of a storm
Or the eye trapped in the window of the boat.
You could begin a series of self-portraits—The Boat
In the Eye of the Remorseful Painter, The Boat in the Eye
Of the Blissful Painter, The Boat in the Eye of the Blind Painter,
The Boat in the Lazy Painter Forgetting His Eye.

Finally one day when the boat's lines are drawn in completely,
It will begin to move away, gradually changing its size,
Enlarging the ocean, requiring less sky, and suddenly it might seem
That you are the one moving. You are the one altering space,
Gliding easily over rough surfaces toward the mark
Between the ocean and the sky. You might see clearly,
For the first time, the boat inside the painter inside the boat
Inside the eye watching the painter moving beyond himself.
You must remember for us the exact color and design of that.

BEING ACCOMPLISHED

Balancing on her haunches, the mouse can accomplish
Certain things with her hands. She can pull the hull
From a barley seed in paperlike pieces the size of threads.
She can turn and turn a crumb to create smaller motes
The size of her mouth. She can burrow in sand and grasp
One single crystal grain in both of her hands.
A quarter of a dried pea can fill her palm.

She can hold the earless, eyeless head
Of her furless baby and push it to her teat.
The hollow of its mouth must feel like the invisible
Confluence sucking continually deep inside a pink flower.

And the mouse is almost compelled
To see everything. Her hand, held up against the night sky,
Can scarcely hide Venus or Polaris
Or even a corner of the crescent moon.
It can cover only a fraction of the blue moth's wing.
Its shadow could never mar or blot enough of the evening
To matter.

Imagine the mouse with her spider-sized hands
Holding to a branch of dead hawthorn in the middle
Of the winter field tonight. Picture the night pressing in
Around those hands, forced, simply by their presence,
To fit its great black bulk exactly around every hair
And every pinlike nail, forced to outline perfectly
Every needle-thin bone without crushing one, to carry
Its immensity right up to the precise boundary of flesh
But no farther. Think how the heavy weight of infinity,
Expanding outward in all directions forever, is forced,

Nevertheless, to mold itself right here and now
To every peculiarity of those appendages.

And even the mind, capable of engulfing
The night sky, capable of enclosing infinity,
Capable of surrounding itself inside any contemplation,
Has been obliged, for this moment, to accommodate the least
Grasp of that mouse, the dot of her knuckle, the accomplishment
Of her slightest intent.

. . . . .

INSIDE GOD'S EYE

As if his eye had no boundaries, at night
All the heavens are visible there. The stars drift
And hesitate inside that sphere like white seeds
Sinking in a still, dark lake. Spirals of brilliance,
They float silently and slowly deeper and deeper
Into the possible expansion of his acuity.
And within that watching, illumination like the moon
Is uncovered petal by petal as a passing cloud clears
The open white flowers of the shining summer plum.

Inside god's eye, light spreads as afternoon spreads,
Accepting the complications of water burr and chestnut,
The efforts of digger bee and cuckoo bee. Even the barest
Light gathers and concentrates there like a ray
Of morning reaching the thinnest nerve of a fairy shrimp
At the center of a pond. And like evening, light
Bends inside the walls of god's eye to make
Skywide globes of fuchsia and orange, violet-tipped
Branches and violet-tinged wings set against a red dusk.

Lines from the tangle of dodder, bindweed
And honeysuckle, from the interweaving knot
Of seaweed and cones, patterns from the network
Of blowing shadow and flashing poplar, fill
And define the inner surface moment of his retina.

And we, we are the only point of reversal
Inside his eye, the only point of light
That turns back on itself and by that turning
Saves time from infinity and saves motion
From obscurity. We are the vessel and the blood
And the pulse he sees as he sees the eye watching
The vision inside his eye in the perfect mirror
Held constantly before his face.

LEGENDARY PERFORMANCE (1987)

NAKED BOYS ON NAKED PONIES

They ride through invisible hollows
And along the indefinite edges of marshy streams,
Fog swirling up to their ears
Over beds of sida and flowering spurge.
The ponies' withers become ivory with pollen
From the blossoming quince, and the bare
Legs of the boys are marked by flickertail
Barley and wild mint. Moisture
On the corn cockle along the ridges
Makes constant suns in their eyes.

Galloping through forests and across fields
Of drying grasses, this is what they create
By themselves—spilled ginseng and screeching
Pipits, dusts rising from the witherod
And the wild raisin, an effusion of broken
Beargrass somersaulting skyward
And mouse-ear chickweed kicked high.

And beside the river they see themselves
On the opposite bank following themselves
Through water chestnuts and willow oak, and they see
Themselves threading among the stand of hornbeam

In the forest ahead. Watching from the precipice
Above the canyon at evening, they know the bronze
Ponies and their riders curving in a line
Along the ledges below.

And at night they see themselves riding upside down
Across the sky, hair and tails and manes
Dragging in the grasses among the long horn beetles
And burrowing owls. And they see themselves galloping
Across the prairie turned upside down, hair
And tails and manes dragging in the dusty glow
Of the starry nebulae. They know they are the definite
Wish of all unexplored spaces to be ponies and boys.

I tell you the speed of the ponies depends absolutely
On the soaring of the rider squeezing tightly
Inside each of their skulls. And the wings of the boys
Depend absolutely on the flight of the ponies
Galloping across the prairies contained in their bones.
And the soaring of the prairies depends absolutely
On the wings of the ponies squeezing tightly
Inside every grass and bone found in the flight of the boys.

And who cares where they are going,
And who cares if they are real or not,
When their ride by itself is that glorious?

. . . . .

A SEASONAL TRADITION

Felicia's music teacher gives a concert for Sonia,
Cecil, Albert, Gordon and Felicia and her insane uncle
In the front parlor every holiday season.
After her traditional repertoire she always plays

One piece on her violin in a register so high
The music can't be heard.

The silence of the parlor during that piece
Is almost complete, broken only by the sputter
Of a candle, a creaking yawn from one of the dogs.

Albert admires the entranced look
On the music teacher's face and the curious trembling
Form of her fingers as she plays. He thinks
He can hear the unheard music in the same way he can hear
Wind among the black strings of the icy willows blowing
In the tundra night. He thinks the silence he hears
Is the same silence found in the eyes of the frogs living
Below the mud at the bottom of the frozen bays.

With tears in her eyes, Felicia says the unheard song
Reminds her of the cries of unborn rice rats
And bog lemmings buried in the winter marsh
And the humming of the white hobblebush blossom still
In its seed and the trill of the unreal bird discovered
In the river trees by the river sun.

Watching the violinist swaying in her velvet gown,
Closing her eyes, pursing her lips, Cecil knows
Sonia is the only possible theme of this composition.

Hoping for a cure for Felicia's uncle, Sonia thinks
The inaudible music might be the unspoken speech
In which he is thought to have lost himself years ago.

At the conclusion of the piece (signaled
By the lowering of the violin) there is always spontaneous
Applause and much barking and leaping by the dogs.

The unheard composition is the one song
Most discussed later over tea and pastries,
And, although it was the subject of the quarrel
During which Cecil knocked Albert's doughnut
From his hand last year, it is still generally considered
The evening's greatest success.

.   .   .   .   .

THE MIRROR OF PIERROT

For Felicia and the unrealized soul of her favorite lost doll

He should never have been set down all alone
In the field like that, a real clown in his floppy
Satin pajamas, dizzy among the trembling pipewort,
Quavering like the brainless wool grass.
Bone-bald in his black skull cap, perpetual
Astonishment on his white painted face, he sits
And stares, his dark lashes as large as teardrops
Circling each wide eye.

How can he ignore the big clicking buttons
Swinging on his baggy blouse as he bends to pick
A prickly daisy for his lapel, or his long cuffs
Falling into the creek as he studies the bravado
Of a crawdad backing under a leaf? Tripped
On the hill by his own pantaloons, he's already lost
One of his tassel-topped silk slippers in a hedgehog hole.

And the starched ruffle around his neck scratches
His ear as he turns to count the jays screaming
Their nonsense among the awkward oaks. He's been teased
For half an hour by a light-headed butterfly flitting
Just out of reach above the raspberry blooms.

Recognizing himself, doesn't he see the wild pantaloons
On the catapulting locust, the bone-tight caps
Of the blackbirds, the white painted faces of the trillium?
He knows the figure he makes sprawled
Among the addle-headed grasses, beside the dumbstruck
Rocks, bewildered under the blank and foolish sky.
He's certain the field is a clumsy buffoon.

Oh, if he could only remember or if he could only
Forget or if he could only imagine someone
Out of sight beyond the hill,
Someone who thinks about him always,
Without laughing.

. . . . .

LOCATING THE SOURCE OF INTENTION

Within the crystal bird that Felicia is admiring
In the window of the curio shop this morning
Is a perfect skeleton of glass bones. The moment
Of the bird's intention to fly appears as a bend
Of purple light curved deep within its wing.
And beneath its glass clavicle is a dram
Of saltwater wavering and shimmering like a heart.

As Felicia looks closer she can see, inside the bubble
Of the bird's body, a transparent egg holding a perfect curl
Of unborn bird, its bones folded as glistening wing
And femur of glass threads. Beneath the vestige of clavicle
There is a sure but wavering salt-point of light.

Looking further she can see, within the loins
Of that unborn bird, a semblance of egg containing
A skeleton of spider-bird bones, a shimmer

Of purple veins connected like night and a hair-bone
Of light forming as heaven's intention to rise like a wing.

And inside the glistening drop of potential egg floating
Inside that embryo-to-be nestled inside the unborn
Bird folded inside the glass bird inside the shop window,
Felicia can sense a definite breath of bones, a waver
Of night wing and a microscopic explosion of light rising
In her eye as proof of the intention
Of a non-existent heart to see.

Felicia is counting backwards now to discover
How many deaths and how many births will be needed
To fully release that flight.

No one knows where the shop owner finds
Such curios to display behind his window
Or how he locates the glassblower
Who executes them.

. . . . .

GENTLEMEN OF LEISURE

Yesterday Felicia put an invitation
In the evening newspaper addressed
To all true Gentlemen of Leisure:

>   Please come tomorrow for an afternoon
>   Of sedate conversation, coffee,
>   Mints and finger croissants.

As the gentlemen arrive, ringing
Once at mid-afternoon, all is prepared.
They place their kid gloves, their chapeaux

And their canes, without clatter, on the marble stand
And proceed to the parlor to seat themselves
On the couch of bruised-rose brocade, the white-lacquered
Chairs and the maroon-cushioned settee.

Felicia thinks the Gentlemen of Leisure
Are magnificently regal in their lavender
Lamb's wool suits and pearl buttons. She adores
Their subtle aromas of unsmoked tobacco, crushed marjoram
And black cinnamon stem.

There are prolonged silences in the parlor
As the gentlemen nod to one another and muse
And abstractly balance their demitasse. They touch
Their temples occasionally with the lace
Of their wine-colored cravats.

They discuss for a moment the brief verse
They discussed during their visit last year.
And they note the shadow of the fern
In its bamboo stand on the dark polished floor.
They recall the rare virgin canary
Which eats small white seeds in the forest
And sips single drops of silver water
In the afternoon and again at dawn.

All true Gentlemen of Leisure are genuinely
And exquisitely calm inside the outer trappings
Of their serenity. Unlike Eduard, who hypocritically
Preaches the code common to all Gentlemen of Leisure,
They know nothing personally of biological
Petulance or preordained harangue.

Cecil wants to paint a portrait
Of the gentlemen sitting and gazing together
In the parlor, but he cannot find the proper shade

Of mauve. And he feels, besides, that the vulgar
Movements of his brush might irreparably violate
The sensitivities of his subjects.

This afternoon, Kioka has insisted
On erecting his sweat-bath tipi on the lawn
Beside the parlor windows. Even though Felicia closes
The drapes, Kioka can still be heard chanting
In the sizzling and sputtering steam that rises
From the glowing rocks. What a triumph
That only one teaspoon rattles against its saucer
As Kioka rushes suddenly from his bath
Screaming his surrender and runs toward the lake!

Doesn't each Gentleman of Leisure sleep well at night,
Cool and scented with rosebay on the smoothest white
Linen, under a coverlet of combed angora, a low light
Burning by his bed in a cut crystal bowl all night?

Sonia must pray for all true Gentlemen of Leisure
Who lend such glorious affirmation
To passivity.

When they rise to leave, precisely
At the perfect moment of dusk, they hold
Their carved canes lightly and stroll
On the white-pebbled path, slowly through the fog
Just gathering among the budding laurel and the full-flowered
Plum, glancing once this way and once that,
And Felicia holds her breath for the beauty.

THE PURSUIT AS SOLUTION

Whenever Albert is bored, he says he wants to know
What's on the other side of the mind. He says
He sometimes has a vision of himself entering
A bird's throat without injuring it, descending
Deeper and deeper headfirst into that warm black center
Until the pressure building at his feet begins to pull
The whole meadow in behind him, every hop clover
And feather foil and smartweed and swamp candle.
And then the hills follow with their grey-green rocks,
Their shagbarks, bitternuts, sourwoods and birches.
And the iron fence around the lawn and the latticed
Arbor house are sucked in too and the warm perfume
Of guests for dinner, crystal salt shakers,
Embroidered napkins. The whole evening sky
Is taken as if it were a net filled with lapping honey bees,
Bot flies, horntails, shrikes and scaups. And even his dreams
Of flying wingless into space and the invisible and the unlikely
And finally light itself are funneled in. Then the bird,
In that vacuum remaining, begins to enter its own throat,
Followed by Albert himself diving in behind himself
And Albert's mind turned inside out.

Sonia thinks Albert should pick
One small thing such as a ceramic thimble
Or a brass button from his great-great-granduncle's
Naval uniform or a six-spotted fishing spider
And try to find the other side of that first,
For practice.

Albert is happy with this suggestion, and now,
On this Tuesday afternoon, he isn't bored any longer
But is out searching along the seashore for a perfect
Short-spined sea urchin or a spiral-tufted

Bryozoan or a trumpet worm or a sea mouse
With which to begin.

Gordon says this whole idea is ridiculous.
Once Albert *knows* what's on the other side of his mind,
It won't be on the other side any longer.

.   .   .   .   .

HOW THE WHALE FORGETS
THE LOVE OF FELICIA

If he breaches at all, he only rises
To a moderate height, rolls little
And falls without luster or surf, silently
In an unremarkable mid-autumn fog.

He rejects the underlying form
Of the fairy shrimp, will not ingest
Fleeing krill if their silver bodies sparkle,
Ignores the possibilities in the strong,
White wings of the manta ray.

In order to avoid the awareness
Of her absence, he must not close his eyes.
In order to avoid the sound of her name,
He must not remind himself to forget.

He deliberately pulls away and bypasses
Brilliant bars of green sun shimmering
Through the dark sea, and he pulls away and sinks
Deliberately from the light salt-vacancies
Of stars ascending like tiny jewels of air
Through the ocean night.

And he never pictures the beauty of barefoot
Riders on horseback when white gulls perch
And flutter on his crusty hump.
And he never remembers tireless dancers
In transparent silks when white waves leap,
Reaching and bowing before a violet sky.

As he moves forward, he doesn't heed or acknowledge
The only direction manifested naturally and forever
Inside the tough hide of his heart, and he doesn't name
The honor of his own broad brow or the honor
Of the comb jellies he passes or the bravery of the bream
And the halfbeaks or the cruelty of the moon's soft skin
Sliding along his own in the night.

How careful he must be never to profess with fervor
The devotion of denial, the clear affirmation
Of suffering.

Indifferent to his own methods, he merely dives
Repeatedly to a depth of dull twilight
Where he meditates without passion on the great
Indeterminable presence of the steady sea, the rock
And return, the capture and simultaneous release
Of its thousand, thousand meaningless caresses.

.   .   .   .   .

THE MYTH: *RAISON D'ÊTRE*

Some say there are wild white ponies
Being washed clean in a clear pool
Beneath a narrow falls in the middle
Of the deciduous forest existing
At the center of the sun.

Some say the thrashing of those ponies
Straining against their bridles, the water flying
From their stamping hooves in fiery pieces
And streaks rising higher than the sandbar willows
Along the bank, drops whirling like sparks
From the manes of their shaking heads,
And the shouting and splashing of the boys
Yanked off their feet by the ponies
As they attempt to wash the great shoulders
And rumps of those rearing beasts, as they lather
Their necks and breasts, stroking them,
Soothing them—all this is the source
Of the fierce binding and releasing energy
Existing at the core of the sun.

The purple jays, mad with the chaos,
Shrieking in the tops of the planetrees,
The rough-winged swallows swerving back
And forth in distress, the struggle of the boys
To soap the inner haunch, to reach
Beneath the belly, to dodge the sharp
Pawing hooves, the wide-eyed screaming
Of the slipping ponies being maneuvered
For the final rinse under the splattering falls—
All the fury of this frightening drama,
Some believe, is contained and borne steadily
Across the blue sky strictly by the startling
Light and combustion of its own commotion.

But when those ponies stand, finally quiet,
Their pure white manes and tails braided
With lilac and rock rose, the boys asleep
On their backs, when they stand,
Fragrant and shimmering, their forelocks
Damp with sweet oil, serene and silent
In the motionless dark of the deep
Riverside forest, then everyone can

Easily see and understand the magnificent
Silhouette, the restrained power, the adorned,
Unblemished and abiding beauty
That is the night.

.   .   .   .   .

THE CREATION OF SIN

Gordon wants to commit a sin
Never committed before. He says he is bored
By the lascivious; he has slept through
A thousand adulteries. He calls theft
And murder and greed embarrassingly unimaginative.

He spends an hour each clear afternoon
On the lawn beneath the alders, grooming the dogs,
Trying to imagine a sin so novel
It has not yet been forbidden.

Sometimes, in the moment just before he discerns
The fish treading in light at the bottom
Of the spring or when he studies the eye
Of the short-eared owl in the instant before it sees
The shrew, he is certain he has already committed
That peculiar sin without knowing it. In the early morning,
As he watches himself from the icy black cedars
By the window, dreaming in his sleep, he can almost
Define it.

As the sole author of a sin,
Gordon knows he would be obligated to create
Its expiation by himself. Grace by seaside scrutiny
He might claim, forgiveness by clam classification,
Confession by continual shell collection.
He could invent sacred vows—sworn custodian

Of conifers, promised caretaker of ambush bugs
And toad bugs. He could preach atonement by paper
And mathematics, redemption by ritual
Guessing at the matter of stars.

Today he has recorded a unique grassland prayer
On a tape with the whooping cranes. He has gathered
Sacraments of metamorphic meal moths and hardening
Sassafras fruit. And he knows if he could just commit
A truly original sin, it would mean the beginning
Of his only real salvation.

.   .   .   .

SIGHT AND SOUND

Kioka rides his brown spotted pinto with naked boys
On naked ponies. They were his darlings
From the beginning, his darlings. Their stomachs
Pressed to the ponies' warm backs, their bare
Heels kicking, every one of them rides fast
With both hands free. Nothing will stop them.
They have the whole wide flat prairie of flowering bluet
Before the house, and they have the whole wide shining
Shore of sand before the sea.

Sonia, Gordon and Albert hurry to the second-story
Veranda to watch the naked boys on their ponies
Whenever they gallop past.

Gordon is pleased to discover that the dark
Blind column of the porch where he places his hand
For a moment contains all the knowledge anyone could pursue
Concerning the galloping hooves of ponies bounding
Over a blue prairie with naked boys on their backs.

Even though Felicia is asleep on a distant hillside
And cannot see or hear the ponies, still it is Kioka
Riding with naked boys who makes the only wide prairie
Of Felicia's heart. It is Kioka who gallops without stopping
Along the only wide shining shore of her heart.

Sonia wants to bring the blind beggars
To the second-story veranda when the ponies pass
So that they may watch the wind coming
Through those flower-filled manes to blow
Against their faces, so that they can see, thereby,
The course of their only cure. And she wants the deaf
Beggars to come and grip the prairie-filled porch railing
During that passing so that they may hear
The only method of their healing.

As the ponies pass, Albert, having removed
All his clothes, stands with his eyes closed
And his ears stopped and grips the column
Of the porch as he rises simultaneously and leaves
The second-story veranda to gallop past himself
On a wild pinto pony following Kioka toward the sea.

Cecil has climbed to the highest garret of the house
So that he can see how Kioka and his ponies reach the bay,
How nothing on the sky or the shore hesitates
As they continue straight out over the water, galloping
Across the waves, through the light-filled spray,
Their hooves striking hard against the flat sun on the surface
Of the sea, how they ride high above the deep, becoming
A rearing surging line of ocean rim racing along the sky.
He leans forward watching them into the evening, watching
Until they pass so far out of sight that he can hear them clearly,
Screaming and thundering and roaring at his back.

SPLITTING AND BINDING (1989)

THE NEXT STORY

All morning long
they kept coming back, the jays,
five of them, blue-grey, purple-banded,
strident, disruptive. They screamed
with their whole bodies from the branches
of the pine, tipped forward, heads
toward earth, and swept across the lawn
into the oleanders, dipping low
as they flew over the half-skull
and beak, the blood-end of the one wing
lying intact, over the fluff
of feathers scattered and drifting
occasionally, easily as dandelion—
all that the cat had left.

Back and forth, past one another,
pausing as if listening, then sharply
cutting the morning again into shard
upon shard of frantic and crested descent,
jagged slivers of raucous outrage,
they kept at it, crying singly, together,
alternately, as if on cue, discordant

anthem. The pattern of their inconsolable
fear could be seen against the flat
spring sky as identical to the pattern
made by the unmendable shatter
of disjointed rubbish on the lawn,
all morning long.

Mothers, fathers, our kind, tell me again
that death doesn't matter. Tell me
it's just a limitation of vision, a fold
of landscape, a deep flax-and-poppy-filled
gully hidden on the hill, a pleat
in our perception, a somersault of existence,
natural, even beneficent, even a gift,
the only key to the red-lacquered door
at the end of the hall, "water
within water," those old stories.

But this time, whatever is said,
when it's said, will have to be more
reverent and more rude, more absolute,
more convincing than these five jays
who have become the five wheeling spokes
and stays of perfect lament, who, without knowing
anything, have accurately matched the black
beaks and spread shoulders of their bodies
to all the shrill, bird-shaped histories
of grief; will have to be demanding enough,
subtle enough, shocking enough, sovereign
enough, right enough to rouse me, to move me
from this window where I have pressed
my forehead hard against the unyielding pane,
unyielding all morning long.

THE DEAD NEVER FIGHT
AGAINST ANYTHING

It's always been that way.
They've allowed themselves to be placed,
knees to chin, in the corners of caves
or in holes in the earth, then covered
with stones; they've let their fingers
be curled around old spears or diadems
or favorite dolls, the stems
of cut flowers.

Whether their skulls were cracked open
and their brains eaten by kin
or whether their brains were pulled
by tongs through their nostrils
and thrown into the dog's dish as waste
are matters that have never concerned them.

They have never offered resistance
to being tied to rocks below the sea,
left for days and nights until their flesh
washed away or likewise to being placed
high in jungle trees or high on scaffolds
alone in the desert until buzzards,
vultures and harpy eagles stripped
their bones bare. They have never minded
jackals nosing at their haunches,
coyotes gnawing at their breasts.

The dead have always been so purely
tolerant. They've let their bones
be rubbed with ointments, ornamented
with ochre, used as kitchen ladles
and spoons. They've been imperturbably

indifferent to the removal of all
their entrails, the resulting cavities
filled with palm wine, aromatic
spices; they have lain complacently
as their abdomens were infused
by syringe with cedar oil.
They've allowed all seven
natural openings of their bodies
to be closed with gold dust.

They've been shrunken and their mouths
sewn shut; they've been wrapped
in gummed linen, corded, bound upright
facing east, hung above coals
and smoked, their ears stuffed
with onions, sent to sea on flaming
pyres. Not one has ever given
a single sign of dissent.

Oblivious to abuse. Even today,
you can hit them and pinch them
and kick them. You can shake them,
scream into their ears. You can cry.
You can kiss them and whisper and moan,
smooth their combed and parted hair, touch
the lips that yesterday spoke, beseech,
entreat with your finest entreaty.
Still, they stare without deviation,
straight into distance and direction.
Old stumps, old shameless logs, rigid
knurls, snow-faced, pitiless,
pitiless betrayal.

During the dearth and lack of those two thousand
Million years of death, one wished primarily
Just to grasp tightly, to compose, to circle,
To link and fasten skillfully, as one
Crusty grey bryozoan builds upon another,
To be *anything* particular, flexing and releasing
In controlled spasms, to make boundaries--replicating
Chains, membranes, epitheliums--to latch on with power
As hooked mussels now adhere to rocky beaches;
To roll up tightly, fistlike, as a water possum,
Spine and skin, curls against the cold;
To become godlike with transformation.

And in that time one eventually wished,
With the dull swell and fall of the surf, to rise up
Out of oneself, to move straight into the violet
Billowing of evening as a willed structure of flight
Trailing feet, or by six pins to balance
Above the shore on a swollen blue lupine, tender,
Almost sore with sap, to shimmer there,
Specific and alone, two yellow wings
Like splinters of morning.

One yearned simultaneously to be invisible,
In the way the oak toad is invisible among
The ashy debris of the scrub-forest floor;
To be grandiose as deserts are grandiose
With punctata and peccaries, Joshua tree,
Saguaro and the mule-ears blossom; to be precise
As the long gleaming hairs of the gourami, swaying
And touching, find the moss and roughage
Of the pond bottom with precision; to stitch
And stitch (that dream) slowly and exactly

As a woman at her tapestry with needle and thread
Sews each succeeding canopy of the rain forest
And with silver threads creates at last
The shining eyes of the capuchins huddled
Among the black leaves of the upper branches.

One longed to be able to taste the salt
Of pity, to hold by bones the stone of grief,
To take in by acknowledgment the light
Of spring lilies in a purple vase, five white
Birds flying before a thunderhead, to become
Infinite by reflection, announcing out loud
In one's own language, by one's own voice,
The fabrication of these desires, this day
Of their recitation.

.   .   .   .   .

THE ORIGIN OF ORDER

Stellar dust has settled.
It is green underwater now in the leaves
Of the yellow crowfoot. Its potentialities
Are gathered together under pine litter
As emerging flower of the pink arbutus.
It has gained the power to make itself again
In the bone-filled egg of osprey and teal.

One could say this toothpick grasshopper
Is a cloud of decayed nebula congealed and perching
On his female mating. The tortoise beetle,
Leaving the stripped veins of morning-glory vines
Like licked bones, is a straw-colored swirl
Of clever gases.

At this moment there are dead stars seeing
Themselves as marsh and forest in the eyes
Of muskrat and shrew, disintegrated suns
Making songs all night long in the throats
Of crawfish frogs, in the rubbings and gratings
Of the red-legged locust. There are spirits of orbiting
Rock in the shells of pointed winkles
And apple snails, ghosts of extinct comets caught
In the leap of darting hare and bobcat, revolutions
Of rushing stone contained in the sound of these words.

Maybe the paths of the Pleiades and Coma clusters
Have been compelled to mathematics by the mind
Contemplating the nature of itself
In the motions of stars. The pattern
Of the starry summer night might be identical
To the structure of the summer heavens circling
Inside the skull. I can feel time speeding now
In all directions deeper and deeper into the black oblivion
Of the electrons directly behind my eyes.

Child of the sky, ancestor of the sky, the mind
Has been obligated from the beginning
To create an ordered universe
As the only possible proof
Of its own inheritance.

.   .   .   .   .

THE ANSWERING OF PRAYERS

Because they have neither tongue
Nor voice, the iris are thought by some
Never to pray, also because they have no hands
To press together and because, born blind,
They cannot properly direct their eyes

Heavenward and, not insignificantly,
Because their god has no ears.

Rising simply from the cement
Of their bulbs, the iris have no premeditated
Motion. They never place one appendage
Deliberately before another in a series
Crossing space. How can they ever formulate, then,
A progress of thought moving from "want"
To "request," from "delight" to "blessing"?
How can they invent what they cannot envision––
A structure of steps leading from "self"
To "beyond"?

Consequently, and some may call it prayer,
They engage themselves in one steady proclamation
Which eventually becomes arched and violet
With petals, pertinently stemmed, budded
With nuance, a subtlety of lissome blades, a sound
Undoubtedly recognized by that deaf god
Who contains within his breast, like the sky-half
Of a spring afternoon, vacancies shaped
As missing floral clusters, purple-streaked
Intimacies. As rooted in his place as April,
It is *their* god who, standing hollow, precedes them
With the absence of brown-wine and lavender bouquets,
Ivory flags on grey-green stalks.

And in the unfolding act of his being filled,
As he becomes weighted, suffused with blossoms
And fragrance, as he feels his heart cupped
And pressed with the intensity of ascent,
In that act of being filled (perfect
Absolution) doesn't he surround, doesn't
He enable, doesn't he with fitting eloquence
Reply?

THE IMPORTANCE OF THE WHALE
IN THE FIELD OF IRIS

They would be difficult to tell apart, except
That one of them sails as a single body of flowing
Grey-violet and purple-brown flashes of sun, in and out
Across the steady sky. And one of them brushes
Its ruffled flukes and wrinkled sepals constantly
Against the salt-smooth skin of the other as it swims past,
And one of them possesses a radiant indigo moment
Deep beneath its lidded crux into which the curious
Might stare.

In the early morning sun, however, both are equally
Colored and silently sung in orange. And both gather
And promote white prairie gulls which call
And circle and soar about them, diving occasionally
To nip the microscopic snails from their brows.
And both intuitively perceive the patterns
Of webs and courseways, the identical blue-glass
Hairs of connective spiders and blood
Laced across their crystal skin.

If someone may assume that the iris at midnight sways
And bends, attempting to focus the North Star
Exactly at the blue-tinged center of its pale stem,
Then someone may also imagine how the whale rolls
And turns, straining to align inside its narrow eye
At midnight, the bright star-point of Polaris.

And doesn't the iris, by its memory of whale,
Straighten its bladed leaves like rows of baleen
Open in the sun? And doesn't the whale, rising
To the surface, breathe by the cupped space
Of the iris it remembers inside its breast?

If they hadn't been found naturally together,
Who would ever have thought to say: The lunge
Of the breaching whale is the fragile dream
Of the spring iris at dawn; the root of the iris
Is the whale's hard wish for careful hands finding
The earth on their own?

It is only by this juxtaposition we can know
That someone exceptional, in a moment of abandon,
Pressing fresh iris to his face in the dark,
Has taken the whale completely into his heart;
That someone of abandon, in an exceptional moment,
Sitting astride the whale's great sounding spine,
Has been taken down into the quiet heart
Of the iris; that someone imagining a field
Completely abandoned by iris and whale can then see
The absence of an exceptional backbone arching
In purple through dark flowers against the evening sky,
Can see how that union of certainty which only exists
By the heart within the whale within the flower rising
Within the breaching heart within the heart centered
Within the star-point of the field's only buoyant heart
Is so clearly and tragically missing there.

.   .   .   .   .

FOR THE WREN TRAPPED IN
A CATHEDRAL

She can never remember how she entered--
What door, what invisible gate, what mistaken
Passage. But in this place every day,
The day shines as a muted mosaic of impenetrable
Colors, and during the black moonless nights,
Every flickering star lifts smoke, drips wax.

She flies, back and forth through the nave, small,
Bewildered among the forest of branchless trees,
Their straight stone trunks disappearing majestically
Into the high arches of the seasonless stone sky.
No weather here, except the predictable weather
Of chant and procession; no storm, except the storm
Of the watchdogs let loose inside at night.

Now when she perches on the bishop's throne
Her song naturally imitates the pattern
Of frills and flutes found in the carvings there,
The hanging fruit, profuse foliage, ripened
Curves. Her trills have adapted themselves
To fit perfectly the detailed abundance
Of that wooden Paradise.

And she has come to believe in gods, swerving close
To the brightness of the apse, attempting to match
Her spread wings, her attitude, to that of the shining
Dove caught there in poised flight above the Ark.
Near the window of the upper chapel, she imagines
She is that other bird, emanating golden rays
To the Christ in the river below.

Resting on a colonnade opposite the south wall
Of stained glass, she watches how the lines
Of her wings become scarlet and purple
With Mary's Grief. And when she flies the entire
Length of the side aisles, she passes
Through the brown-orange swath of light
From the Journey into Egypt, the green and azure
Of the Miracle of the Five Thousand Fed.
Occasionally she finds that particular moment
And place where she is magnificently transformed,
The dull brown of her breast becoming violet
And magenta with the Adoration of the Magi.

What is it that happens to her body, to bone
And feather and eye, when, on some dark evenings,
She actually sees herself covered, bathed, suffused
In the red blood of the Crucifixion?

Among the statues at night, she finds it a peace,
A serenity, to pause, to murmur in sleep
Next to the ear of a saint, to waken
Nested on the outstretched hand
Of the Savior's unchanging blessing.

Certainly she dreams often of escape, of reversing
That process by which she came to be here, leaving
As an ordinary emissary carrying her own story,
Sacred news from the reality of artifice,
Out into the brilliant white mystery
Of the truthful world.

. . . . .

THERE IS A WAY TO
WALK ON WATER

Over the elusive, blue salt-surface easily,
Barefoot, and without surprise—there is a way
To walk far above the tops of volcanic
Scarps and mantle rocks, towering seamounts
Rising in peaks and rifts from the ocean floor,
Over the deep black flow of that distant
Bottom as if one walked studiously
And gracefully on a wire of time
Above eternal night, never touching
Fossil reef corals or the shells of leatherbacks,
Naked gobies or the crusts of sea urchins.

There is a way to walk on water,
And it has something to do with the feel
Of the silken waves sliding continuously
And carefully against the inner arches
Of the feet; and something to do
With what the empty hands, open above
The weed-blown current and chasm
Of that possible fall, hold to tightly;
Something to do with how clearly
And simply one can imagine a silver scatter
Of migrating petrels flying through the body
During that instant, gliding with their white
Wings spread through the cartilage of throat
And breast, across the vast dome of the skull,
How distinctly one can hear them calling singly
And together inside the lungs, sailing straight
Through the spine as if they themselves believed
That bone and moment were passageways
Of equal accessibility.

Buoyant and inconsequential, as serious,
As exact as stone, that old motion of the body,
That visible stride of the soul, when the measured
Placing of each toe, the perfect justice
Of the feet, seems a sublimity of event,
A spatial exaltation--to be able to walk
Over water like that has something to do
With the way, like a rain-filled wind coming
Again to dry grasses on a prairie, all
Of these possibilities are remembered at once,
And the way, like many small blind mouths
Taking drink in their dark sleep,
All of these powers are discovered,
Complete and accomplished
And present from the beginning.

KNOT

Watching the close forest this afternoon
and the riverland beyond, I delineate
quail down from the dandelion's shiver
from the blowzy silver of the cobweb
in which both are tangled. I am skillful
at tracing the white egret within the white
branches of the dead willow where it roosts
and at separating the heron's graceful neck
from the leaning stems of the blue-green
lilies surrounding. I know how to unravel
sawgrasses knitted to iris leaves knitted
to sweet vernals. I can unwind sunlight
from the switches of the water in the slough
and divide the grey sumac's hazy hedge
from the hazy grey of the sky, the red vein
of the hibiscus from its red blossom.

All afternoon I part, I isolate, I untie,
I undo, while all the while the oak
shadows, easing forward, slowly ensnare me,
and the calls of the wood peewees catch
and latch in my gestures, and the spicebush
swallowtails weave their attachments
into my attitude, and the damp sedge
fragrances hook and secure, and the swaying
Spanish mosses loop my coming sleep,
and I am marsh-shackled, forest-twined,
even as the new stars, showing now
through the night-spaces of the sweet gum
and beech, squeeze into the dark
bone of my breast, take their perfectly
secured stitches up and down, pull
all of their thousand threads tight
and fasten, fasten.

THE FAMILY IS ALL THERE IS

Think of those old, enduring connections
found in all flesh––the channeling
wires and threads, vacuoles, granules,
plasma and pods, purple veins, ascending
boles and coral sapwood (sugar-
and light-filled), those common ligaments,
filaments, fibers and canals.

Seminal to all kin also is the open
mouth––in heart urchin and octopus belly,
in catfish, moonfish, forest lily,
and rugosa rose, in thirsty magpie,
wailing cat cub, barker, yodeler,
yawning coati.

And there is a pervasive clasping
common to the clan––the hard nails
of lichen and ivy sucker
on the church wall, the bean tendril
and the taproot, the bolted coupling
of crane flies, the hold of the shearwater
on its morning squid, guanine
to cytosine, adenine to thymine,
fingers around fingers, the grip
of the voice on presence, the grasp
of the self on place.

Remember the same hair on pygmy
dormouse and yellow-necked caterpillar,
covering red baboon, thistle seed
and willow herb? Remember the similar
snorts of warthog, walrus, male moose
and sumo wrestler? Remember the familiar
whinny and shimmer found in river birches,

bay mares and bullfrog tadpoles,
in children playing at shoulder tag
on a summer lawn?

The family--weavers, reachers, winders
and connivers, pumpers, runners, air
and bubble riders, rock-sitters, wave-gliders,
wire-wobblers, soothers, flagellators--all
brothers, sisters, all there is.

Name something else.

. . . . .

ROLLING NAKED IN
THE MORNING DEW

Out among the wet grasses and wild barley-covered
Meadows, backside, frontside, through the white clover
And feather peabush, over spongy tussocks
And shaggy-mane mushrooms, the abandoned nests
Of larks and bobolinks, face to face
With vole trails, snail niches, jelly
Slug eggs; or in a stone-walled garden, level
With the stemmed bulbs of orange and scarlet tulips,
Cricket carcasses, the bent blossoms of sweet william,
Shoulder over shoulder, leg over leg, clear
To the ferny edge of the goldfish pond—some people
Believe in the rejuvenating powers of this act—naked
As a toad in the forest, belly and hips, thighs
And ankles drenched in the dew-filled gulches
Of oak leaves, in the soft fall beneath yellow birches,
All of the skin exposed directly to the *killy* cry
Of the king bird, the buzzing of grasshopper sparrows,
Those calls merging with the dawn-red mists

Of crimson steeplebush, entering the bare body then
Not merely through the ears but through the skin
Of every naked person willing every event and potentiality
Of a damp transforming dawn to enter.

Lillie Langtry practiced it, when weather permitted,
Lying down naked every morning in the dew,
With all of her beauty believing the single petal
Of her white skin could absorb and assume
That radiating purity of liquid and light.
And I admit to believing myself, without question,
In the magical powers of dew on the cheeks
And breasts of Lillie Langtry believing devotedly
In the magical powers of early morning dew on the skin
Of her body lolling in purple beds of bird's-foot violets,
Pink prairie mimosa. And I believe, without doubt,
In the mystery of the healing energy coming
From that wholehearted belief in the beneficent results
Of the good delights of the naked body rolling
And rolling through all the silked and sun-filled,
Dusky-winged, sheathed and sparkled, looped
And dizzied effluences of each dawn
Of the rolling earth.

Just consider how the mere idea of it alone
Has already caused me to sing and sing
This whole morning long.

. . . . .

WHEN AT NIGHT

Suppose all of you came in the dark,
each one, up to my bed while I was sleeping;

Suppose one of you took my hand
without waking me and touched my fingers,
moved your lips the length of each one, down
into the crotch with your tongue and up again,
slowly sucking the nipple of each knuckle
with your eyes closed;

Suppose two of you were at my head, the breath
of one in my ear like a bird/moth thuddering
at a silk screen; the other fully engaged, mouth
tasting of sweetmeats and liquors,
kissing my mouth;

Suppose another drew the covers
down to my feet, slipped the loops
from the buttons, spread my gown,
ministering mouth again around the dark
of each breast, pulling and puckering
in the way that water in a stir
pulls and puckers a fallen
bellflower into itself;

Two at my shoulders to ease
the gown away, take it down
past my waist and hips, over my ankles
to the end of the bed; one of you
is made to adore the belly; one of you
is obsessed with dampness; at my bent
knees now, another watching, at my parted
thighs another; and one to oversee
the separation and one to guard the joining
and one to equal my trembling and one
to protect my moaning;

And at dawn, if everything were put
in place again, closing, sealing, my legs

together, straight, the quilt folded
and tucked to my chin; if all of you
stepped back, away, into your places,
into the translucence of glass
at the window, into the ground breezes
swelling the limber grasses, into the river
of insect rubbings below the field and the light
expanding the empty spaces of the elm, back
into the rising black of the hawk deepening
the shallow sky, and we all woke then
so much happier than before, well,
there wouldn't be anything
wrong in that, would there?

. . . . .

FOR PASSIONS DENIED:
PINEYWOODS LILY

Who knows what unrelieved yearning
finally produced the pink-and-lavender-wax control
of these petals, what continual longing
resulted in the sharp arcing of the leaves,
what unceasing obsession became itself
in the steady siren of the ruby stigma? That tense
line of magenta disappearing over the boundaries
of the blossom is so unequivocal in the decision
of its direction, one is afraid to look too long.

I can understand, perhaps, having a hopeless
passion for gliding beneath the sea, wanting to swim
leisurely, without breath, through green salt
and sun-tiered water, to sleep all night, lost
and floating among the stroking of the angelfish,
the weaving rags of the rays. And I can understand
an impossible craving to fly unencumbered,

without effort, naked and easily over sandstone
canyons, through the high rain of river-filled
gorges, to feel the passing pressures of an evening
sky against the forehead, against the breast.
And I can understand the desire to touch a body
that may never be touched, the frenzy to move
one's hand along a thigh into a darkness
which will never have proximity, to take into oneself
the entire perfume, the whole yeast and vibration
and seethe of that which will always remain
aloof, a desire so unrelenting it might easily turn
any blood or pistil at its deepest crux
to majestic purple.

I don't know what it is that a pineywoods lily,
with all her being, might wish for. Yet whatever dearest
thing this lily was denied, it's clear
she must very greatly have suffered, to be before us now
so striking in her bearing, so fearsome
in her rage.

. . . . .

THE OBJECTS OF IMMORTALITY

If I could bestow immortality,
I'd do it liberally—on the aim of the hummingbird,
The sea nettle and the dispersing skeletons of cottonweed
In the wind, on the night heron hatchling and the night heron
Still bound in the blue-green darkness of its egg,
On the thrice-banded crab spider and on every low shrub
And tall teasel stem of its most perfect places.

I would ask that the turquoise skimmer, hovering
Over backwater moss, stay forever, without faltering,
Without disappearing, head half-eaten on the mud, one wing

Under pine rubbish, one floating downstream, nudged
And spit away by foraging darters.

And for that determination to survive,
Evident as the vibration of the manta ray beneath sand,
As the tight concentration of each trout-lily petal
On its stem, as the barbed body curled in the brain
Of the burrowing echidna, for that intensity
Which is not simply the part of the bittern's gold eye
Most easily identified and remembered but the entire
Bittern itself, for that bird-shaped realization
Of effective pressure against oblivion, I would make
My own eternal assertion: Let that pressure endure.

And maybe this immortality can come to pass
Because continuous life, even granted to every firefly
And firebeetle and fireworm on earth, to the glowing clouds
Of every deep-sea squirt, to all electric eels, phosphorescent
Fishes and scaly, bright-bulbed extensions of the black
Ocean bottoms, to all luminous fungi and all torch-carrying
Creatures, to the lost light and reflective rock
Of every star in the summer sky, everlasting life,
Even granted to all of these multiplied a million times,
Could scarcely perturb or bother anyone truly understanding
The needs of infinity.

.   .   .   .   .

BEFORE I WAKE

The turning of the marsh marigold coming slowly
Into its emergent bloom underwater; the turning
Of the coral sands over themselves and over their dunes
And over the scratchings of the scarab beetles
Turning over the dung of the desert doe; the pivoting

Of the eye of the bluefish turning inside the drawing light
Of its multiple school shifting its constellation
In the dark sea; this is the prayer of sleep
In which I lay myself down to dream.

The quiet enclosed by the burrowing wolf spider
Dragging its egg sac to the surface to sun;
The stillness covered by the barren strawberry
Making its fleshless seed on the rocky hill;
The study in the desert mushroom knotting itself
In the arid heat; the silence of the fetal sea horses
Bound in the pouch of their father; this is the dream
Of the soul in which I lay myself down to pray.

And I've asked the outward motion of the hollow web
Of the elm making leaf, and I've asked the inward motion
Of every glinting fin making the focus of the carp,
And I've asked the involution of the egg buds carried
In the dark inside the cowbirds circling overhead,
And I've asked the tight coiling and breaking
Of light traveling in the beads of the sawgrass
And the net of the sea oats splitting and binding
And splitting again over and over across the open lands
To keep me in this dream tonight through one prayer more.

GEOCENTRIC (1993)

A COMMON SIGHT

There is at least one eye
for everything here this afternoon.
The algae and the yeasts, invisible
to some, for instance, are seen
by the protozoa; and the black-tailed
seeds of tadpoles are recognized
on sight by the giant, egg-carrying
water beetle. Brook trout have eyes
for caddisfly larvae, pickerel
for dragonfly nymphs; redfin shiners
bear witness to the presence
of flocks of water fleas.

The grains of the goldenrod
are valued, sought out, found
by the red-legged grasshopper who is,
in turn, noticed immediately
by the short-tailed shrew whose least
flitter alarms and attracts
the rodent-scoped eye
of the white-winged hawk.

There is an eye for everything.
The two-lined salamander watches
for the horsehair worm, as the stilt spider
pays sharp attention to midge fly,
crane fly. The cricket frog
will not pass unnoticed, being spied
specifically by the ringed raccoon,
and, despite the night beneath
the field, the earthworm, the grub
and the leafhopper larva are perceived
by the star-nosed mole.

So odd, that nothing goes unnoticed.
Even time has its testimony,
each copepod in the colony possessing
a red eyespot sensitive to the hour,
the entire congregation rising
as one body at dusk to touch the dark
where it exists above the pond.

And I have an eye myself
for this particular vision, this continuous
validation-by-sight that's given
and taken over and over by clam shrimp,
marsh treader, bobcat, the clover-coveting
honeybee, by diving teal, the thousand-eyed
bot fly, the wild and vigilant,
shadow-seeking mollusk mya.

Watch now, for my sake, how I stalk. Watch
how I secure this vision. Watch how long
and lovingly, watch
how I feed.

IN ADDITION TO FAITH, HOPE, AND CHARITY

I'm sure there's a god
in favor of drums. Consider
their pervasiveness—the thump,
thump and slide of waves
on a stretched hide of beach,
the rising beat and slap
of their crests against shore
baffles, the rapping of otters
cracking mollusks with stones,
woodpeckers beak-banging, the beaver's
whack of his tail-paddle, the ape
playing the bam of his own chest,
the million tickering rolls
of rain off the flat-leaves
and razor-rims of the forest.

And we know the noise
of our own inventions—snare and kettle,
bongo, conga, big bass, toy tin,
timbals, tambourine, tom-tom.

But the heart must be the most
pervasive drum of all. Imagine
hearing all together every tinny
snare of every heartbeat
in every jumping mouse and harvest
mouse, sagebrush vole and least
shrew living across the prairie;
and add to that cacophony the individual
staccato tickings inside all gnatcatchers,
kingbirds, kestrels, rock doves, pine
warblers crossing, crisscrossing

each other in the sky, the sound
of their beatings overlapping
with the singular hammerings
of the hearts of cougar, coyote,
weasel, badger, pronghorn, the ponderous
bass of the black bear; and on deserts too,
all the knackings, the flutterings
inside wart snakes, whiptails, racers
and sidewinders, earless lizards, cactus
owls; plus the clamors undersea, slow
booming in the breasts of beluga
and bowhead, uniform rappings
in a passing school of cod or bib,
the thidderings of bat rays and needlefish.

Imagine the earth carrying this continuous
din, this multifarious festival of pulsing
thuds, stutters and drummings, wheeling
on and on across the universe.

This must be proof of a power existing
somewhere definitely in favor
of such a racket.

.   .   .   .   .

GEOCENTRIC

Indecent, self-soiled, bilious
reek of turnip and toadstool
decay, dribbling the black oil
of wilted succulents, the brown
fester of rotting orchids,
in plain view, that stain
of stinkhorn down your front,
that leaking roil of bracket

fungi down your back, you
purple-haired, grainy-fuzzed
smolder of refuse, fathering
fumes and boils and powdery
mildews, enduring the constant
interruption of sink-mire
flatulence, contagious
with ear wax, corn smut,
blister rust, backwash
and graveyard debris, rich
with manure bog and dry-rot
harboring not only egg-addled
garbage and wrinkled lip
of orange-peel mold but also
the clotted breath of overripe
radish and burnt leek, bearing
every dank, malodorous rut
and scarp, all sulphur fissures
and fetid hillside seepages, old,
old, dependable, engendering
forever the stench and stretch
and warm seeth of inevitable
putrefaction, nobody
loves you as I do.

. . . . .

LIFE AND DEATH: ALL THE LOST
ACCORDIONS AND CONCERTINAS

You may wonder yourself what happened to them.
They're at the bottom of the sea.
Some people saw them floating downward,
discarded, sinking slowly into that foreign plane.

They were humming and chording
all the while, inside a confetti of bubbles,
their bellows expanding, opening
like the folded fins of butterfly fish.
Their leather straps were fluttering
behind them like ribbon fish, writhing
like eels, attached like lampreys.

A cargo of concertinas sailed
the salt surface momentarily, bobbing
like a fleet of air-filled jellyfish.

Down they all went, schools and cities
of them, turning and tumbling,
mother-of-pearl buttons gleaming,
keys and reeds quivering.

They recline there yet where they settled,
half-buried in muddy sand, tilting
on cliffs of coral, bobbled and nosed
by jacks and rays. Their bodies
teeter, bowing, contracting
to the tempo of the surf.
They wheeze and blow nightly
with the currents, singing like sirens,
shimmering in their treble, tenor treble.
Their sound is the same sound
you can imagine hearing if beds of waving
seaweed were a chorus of violins.

They take in and give forth their element.
They breathe and moan, those eternal
lungs. They speak. They are greater
than ghosts.

Their soliloquies circle the wide sea,
rippled and meditative, are heard
by nursing blue whales,
who answer.

. . . . .

GOOD HEAVENS

1.

The common garden snail can't watch
the heavens and enumerate--600 young
stars in Perseus, one more hour
until full moon. It can't make lists--
pinwheel of Andromeda, comet fireball
of Tempel-Tuttle. It has never called
its slither the soft finger of night
nor its wound shell a frozen
galactic spin. Yet its boneless,
thumb-sized head is filled and totally
deaf with exactly the same tone
and timbre as the sky.

2. *WINTER MIDNIGHT*

It seemed I was looking into the face
of a vendor, skin so dark
I couldn't focus at first,
the stark structure of his skull
tighter, blacker even than his eyes.
It was a vendor with his wares--glass
bulbs and seeds, silver goats, loops
and strings of copper, brass-cathedral
charms, polished couples on sticks

copulating, twisted bracelets
and rings—spread like a market
of stars on the blanket at his knees.
I thought I saw borders, ways
and measures in his onyx face.
A shifty hawker, a familiar swindler,
it was an old, skinny vendor on folded
knees, kneeling purple bones, a skeleton
of vestments, a posture of spirals
and stocks hovering above and below
his spread of sockets and hoops,
reaching, rocking, merchandising
at my elbow: *Kum, laydee, bye,*
kum bye mine.

3.

To imagine stars and flaming
dust wheeling inside the gut
of a blind, transparent fish
swimming out of sight in the black
waters of a cave a thousand years ago
is to suggest that the perfect
mystery of time, motion and light
remains perfect.

4.

Good—because the heavy burnings
and fumings of evolving
star clusters and extragalactic
cacophonies—because the flaming
Cygnus Loop, still whipping
and spewing sixty thousand years
after its explosion—because
the churning, disgorging womb

of the Great Nebula and the rushing
oblivions left from the collapse
of protostars—because suffocating
caverns of pulling, sucking gases
and pursuing, encircling ropes
of nuclear bombardments—
because erupting cauldrons
of double stars and multiple
stars flinging outward great
spires and towers of searing
poisons—because all of these
for this long have stayed
far, *far* away from our place.

. . . . .

ELINOR FROST'S MARBLE-TOPPED KNEADING TABLE

Imagine that motion, the turning and pressing,
the constant folding and overlapping, the dough
swallowing and swallowing and swallowing itself
again, just as the sea, bellying up the hard shore,
draws back under its own next forward-moving
roll, slides out from under itself
along the beach and back again; that first
motion, I mean, like the initial act
of any ovum (falcon, leopard, crab) turning
into itself, taking all of its outside surfaces
inward; the same circular mixing and churning
and straightening out again seen at the core
of thunderheads born above deserts; that involution
ritualized inside amaryllis bulbs
and castor beans in May.

Regard those hands now, if you never
noticed before, flour-caked fists and palms knuckling
the lump, gathering, dividing, tucking
and rolling, smoothing, reversing. I know,
from the stirring and sinking habits
of your own passions, that you recognize
this motion.

And far in the distance, (you may even
have guessed) far past Orion and Magellan's vapors,
past the dark nebulae and the sifted rings
of interstellar dust, way beyond mass and propulsion,
before the first wheels and orbits of sleep
and awareness, there, inside that moment
which comes to be, when we remember,
at the only center where it has always been,
an aproned figure stands kneading, ripe
with yeast, her children at her skirts.
Now and then she pauses, bends quickly,
clangs open the door, tosses another stick
on the fire.

.   .   .   .   .

SNOW THINKING

Someone must have thought of snow falling first,
before it happened. That's what I believe,
someone way before me, way before anyone
could write "snow" and then see it happen--
in the cracks between the mud bricks
of the patio, assuming the shapes
of seeded sedum and wineleaf, covering
the tops of overturned flowerpots,

so much whiter than the sky it comes from--
as we do sometimes.

I think it must have come (the being
of the motion of snow, I mean, furling out
of the black, this method of winding
and loosening, this manner of arriving)
first from deep inside someone, as we say,
out of some quiet, exuberant graciousness,
far beyond neutron or electron, way before
eyes or hands, far before any crudeness
like that.

It had to come from someone first,
before snow, *this expression of snow,*
the swift, easy, multi-faceted
passion possessed and witnessed
in descending snow. It must be so.
Otherwise, how could we, as ourselves,
recognize it now--*the event of snow,*
so clearly eloquent, so separate,
so much rarer than *snow?* It's there.
We know it--the succumbing to sky,
the melding, nothing too small
for the embracing, a singular gentleness.

And don't we know now, without seeing it,
without touching it, that outside the window
the snow is coming, accumulating over the walls
and hedges of the garden, covering
the terra cotta, filling all the filigree
and deficiencies of evening?

I believe that snow snowing is the form
of someone singing in the future

to a new and beloved child, a child who,
staring up at the indistinguishable
features of his mother's star-filled face
in the dark, knows, without touching
or seeing, the experience of snow, opening
his mouth to catch and eat every spark
of the story as it breaks and falls
so particularly upon him.

.   .   .   .   .

DISTANCE AND DEPTH

Whether looking down through
a pond's surface, past a brown mossy
tavern of twigs into a floating nest
and through the membrane of a single
translucent egg globule, down
into the drama and complex carnival
of that jelly mote, its lipids,
ashes and crystal inclusions,
through its loops and plots
and domestications, past bound
messages, gates, stringy messengers,
past storms, sparks, signs and orbits,
on down toward the tense purple
nebula of chaos at its core;

or whether watching far out over
the flat grasses and gullies, skimming
the plains past low opuntia, hidden
beeflies, jumping mice, the burrows
of dogs and deer and all that multitude,
right up to the first rising red rock
range and past that to the next sheer

evergreen plateau and on beyond
to the ultimate highest blue snow
of the peaks with names, past them
to the ragged ridge of the sinking moon
and behind that into the easy black
where the eyes seem suddenly turned
hard and fast on themselves;

whether distance or depth, either way
it's evident there are fields and fields
and fields aplenty, more and more
space than is needed, ample space
for any kind of sin to be laid down,
disassembled, swallowed away, lost,
absorbed, forgotten, transformed,
if one should only ask
for such a favor.

.   .   .   .   .

BY DEATH

In that moment she became two, one sitting
among the red flags of the blackbirds
in the reeds, the other standing fixed
like a poplar in a fence of poplars.

In the next second, there were four
of her, one watching evening from the sill
beside the bed, another laced through the night-
spaces between the fireflies.

In a further splitting, she was eight,
and in the next sixteen, one blue

by paper lantern, one amethyst by evening
smoke, one ringed like ice by a winter
moon, one ringed like a lily-pond by rain,
one marked by murder, one veined
by acquittal.

And there were thirty-two of her then
and again sixty-four, and she was simultaneously
over a plain of summer cress and under
a reef of evening coral, within a knob
of shyster thistle, within a bud of thresher
shark, sailing by roots of bony fish,
soaring by fins of tamarack and phlox.

With the next turning she became
a hundred and twenty-eight of herself, groomed
the horse of Orion, dwelled in the light-remnant
of Vela. She was wind through the scaffold
of pity, a nesting owl among the eaves of praise.
Then two hundred fifty-six—she was stone as well,
and zephyr, then legion, then too various
to be reckoned, too pervasive to be noticed,
too specific to be named.

. . . . .

TO COMPLETE A THOUGHT

"In order to define the issue . . ." he begins,
as an orange one leaps from the piano, lands
in the middle of the room on the floral
carpet, bounds again, climbs halfway
up the silk drapes and stops, legs spread,
hanging as if suspended there.

"Time in a timeless . . ." she pauses,
as the calico jumps from her lap, scrambles
up the drapes, chasing the swishing
orange tail of the other.

A short-haired yellow one skids
around the corner, at this point, sliding,
skittering, batting at a rolling bell, jangling
and spinning it down the marble hallway.

"Heredity definitely plays
a role," he replies.

"It's a simple matter of give
and take," she responds, as a grey one falls
from the chandelier, lands on the head
of a tabby, slides off, raking
one ear with a hind claw (just a slight
suggestion of blood).

Two toms race through the open
door at this moment, thud along the couch, fly
from the top of the chintz armchair
to the mantlepiece, spilling a brass jar
of round rum candies.

"Even god as a concept . . ." he continues,
while an old matted white one sips perfumed
water from a vase of camellias
sitting on a buffet before the mirror.

"If we could just catch hold . . ."
she whispers. Three thin black ones,
sitting on the icy windowsill outside, peer
into the parlor with indignant longing.

She sighs, stretches, slowly licks
her finger, wets and winds a neck curl
into place, while he watches,
swaying, hind quarters wriggling
until he pounces, catches and pulls loose
in a sudden release of one motion
the trailing sash of her cashmere robe.

. . . . .

UNDER THE BIG TOP

> *Though I walk through the valley of the shadow . . .*
>
> PSALM 23

They're always here. One of them tumbles
in her maroon and silver-sequined tights before me,
as if she led, down the road. She somersaults, flips
mid-air over a hedge row, her bodice sparkling, over
a patch of butterfly pea. She does handstands
off curbs, cartwheels down alleys, leapfrogs
past parking meters. Crossing any bridge
with her is ceremony, a ritual of back bends
on thin wooden railings, toe-dances
on suspension cables.

How can I fear, one going ahead armed with chair
and fake pistol, two going ahead in epaulettes and brass
buttons, with marching drum, bold tasseled baton?

Another keeps a constant circle of blossoms
and pods spinning around my head. Tossing
and catching, he weaves almonds, apples, limes,
pomegranates, once the spotted eggs of the wood pewee,
once the buds of the Cherokee rose. So deft,
nothing he handles falls or shatters or bruises.

Even in the night far ahead I can see his torches,
their flames spiralling high into the black
dome, down again into his waiting hands.

And this one, such comfort, shuffles at my pace,
following one step behind. Holding his purple
pint-sized parasol above my head, he recovers
from each of his stumbles, tripping over stray dogs,
paper cups, raindrops, stepping on the dragging
cuffs of his own striped trousers. He keeps up,
guffawing when he hears me laugh, stopping abruptly
if I cease. And when he sees tears in my eyes,
he takes out his cowboy hankie, honks his schnoz,
shakes his doleful head, with chin trembling,
presses two sad fingertips sincerely
to his garish grin.

. . . . .

THE YEAR ALL THE CLOWNS WERE EXECUTED

Many saw them taken away, crowded
in the wagons, chained together,
their oblong white faces peering
through the slats, eyebrows arched high
with bewilderment. All those joeys,
some were wearing cup-sized black
bowlers on their bald heads,
others topless top hats
resting on their ears, orange neckties
down to their knees. A few
blew on bubble pipes and pondered
the sky as the wagons bumped along.
One in baggy blue coat, a tin foil

star pinned to his chest, beat
the others repeatedly
with his billy club balloon.

Their painted tears
looked real.

Later, after the last wagon
had disappeared into the mountains,
that was a bad time for all merchants
selling floppy chartreuse satin pajamas
with big ball buttons, tent-sized
trousers of tartan plaid and purple
stripes. The Squirting Plastic
Flower Company and the Six-Inch Bicycle
Factory had to close shop completely.
Fox terriers, trained to wear
bonnets and ride in baby buggies,
lost their jobs. Soon the youngest
children couldn't remember a shivaree,
the parade of stunts, midget cars
or prancing piglets, the "walk-around"
on the Hippodrome track.

Then toward the end of that year,
visionaries began to appear, the first one
claiming to have seen the stiltman at dusk
striding in his gold metallic suit
through a copse of slender prairie
poplars in the shadowy evening sun,
another swearing to have witnessed
Petrolino himself wearing his pointed
hat topped with bells, ducking down
and popping up among the swaying
cattails, frightening all the blackbirds
in the most comical way. A third, watching

a distant field of autumn milkweed,
testified to seeing confetti
fly into the air from the old
empty-water-bucket gag.
Even a grandmother living alone
heard Grimaldi singing "An Oyster
Crossed in Love" beneath the scraping
branches outside her window
just before dawn.

But on a windy evening at midnight,
when a whole party of laughing people
together saw one of their favorites
stumbling on the sidewalk in the bluster,
tripping up the curb, reeling
against a trash can, somersaulting
again headfirst, sprawling
and pitching, taking his pratfalls
down the street like a blowing tangle
of open newspaper, then no one dared
deny any longer the truths
of spirits and souls, that bold new
rumor of resurrection.

. . . . .

GET ON BOARD

While all the seas harass themselves
with whipping waterspouts and typhoons,
while all the seas draw back
out of themselves into still poplar
prairies and sheaths of ice, while Lily,
her spine pressed against the oak, murders

her baby in the forest, and Hubert
at tea time hands Rose a lemon wedge
and cream—all along it continues
to move along, that wagon, its bed
planed and pegged like a floor,
its sides like a farm wagon
slatted and high.

Where the mottled mongrel, chained
to the shed, meets the returning howl
of his own barking at midnight,
where the spotted salamander
at the pond's edge relinquishes
its color and motion to the blooming
milfoil, where the eye of the snow hare,
alone on a white plain, becomes
the only true vortex and blizzard of winter,
there it passes also, creaking
and swaying, the hub of each wheel turning
like a coin spun on a table, each spoke
circling like a lighthouse beacon.

It passes the fallen and fern-cradling
tree from which it is constructed,
passes the ocean valley from which its lumber
will grow, passes the sleeping infant
who has forged its axle, passes the grave
of the smith who will ring its wheels,
passes blind Edith who points and shouts,
"See the flaming wagon crossing the sky,"
passes Uncle Morris reciting, "There lies
the wagon, broken, upside down in the ditch,"
passes itself, sides hung with orchis
and lavender, wheels laced with sage,
inside the visionary's mind.

It sways and rumbles, traveling always
both subsequent and prior to every moment
of its path. Don't you know it? Can't you see?
You, riding along with all of its passengers,
standing up, laughing now, waving
your hat, hallooing and hallooing?

. . . . .

THE PROCESS

First she gave all that she carried
in her arms, setting those trinkets down easily.
Then she removed her scarlet sash and gave it
for bandage, her scarf for blindfold, her shawl,
her handkerchief for shroud.

She let her violet kimono slip from her shoulders,
giving it too, because it was warm and could surround,
enwrap like dusk, and because it held her dark-river,
night-swimmer fragrances tight in the deep
stitches of its seams.

And she cut off her hair, offering its strands
for weaving, for pillow, lining, talisman,
for solace.

She gave her bracelets, the rings
from her fingers—those circles of gold jingling
like crickets, those loops of silver
chiming like spring—and gave her hands as well,
her fingers, the way they could particularize.

Her feet and their balance, her legs
and their stride, she relinquished;

and her belly, her thighs, her lap—wide, empty,
open as a prairie—her breasts full of sunlight,
like peaches and honey, like succor. She gave away
her bones—ribcage for scaffold, spine,
smaller knuckles for kindling, for sparks,
for flame.

And what remained—her face, her visage
reflective, transparent as sky—she gave
and even her word, her name, its echo,
until all, everything was given and everything
received, and she was no one,
gone, nothing,
god.

. . . . .

THE GREATEST GRANDEUR

Some say it's in the reptilian dance
of the purple-tongued sand goanna,
for there the magnificent translation
of tenacity into bone and grace occurs.

And some declare it to be an expansive
desert—solid rust-orange rock
like dusk captured on earth in stone—
simply for the perfect contrast it provides
to the blue-grey ridge of rain
in the distant hills.

Some claim the harmonics of shifting
electron rings to be most rare and some
the complex motion of seven sandpipers

bisecting the arcs and pitches
of come and retreat over the mounting
hayfield.

Others, for grandeur, choose the terror
of lightning peals on prairies or the tall
collapsing cathedrals of stormy seas,
because there they feel dwarfed
and appropriately helpless; others select
the serenity of that ceiling/cellar
of stars they see at night on placid lakes,
because there they feel assured
and universally magnanimous.

But it is the dark emptiness contained
in every next moment that seems to me
the most singularly glorious gift,
that void which one is free to fill
with processions of men bearing burning
cedar knots or with parades of blue horses,
belled and ribboned and stepping sideways,
with tumbling white-faced mimes or companies
of black-robed choristers; to fill simply
with hammered silver teapots or kiln-dried
crockery, tangerine and almond custards,
polonaises, polkas, whittling sticks, wailing
walls; that space large enough to hold all
invented blasphemies and pieties, 10,000
definitions of god and more, never fully
filled, never.

OLD SPIRAL OF CONCEPTION (1994)

(NEW POEMS IN THE ORIGINAL *FIREKEEPER*)

TILL MY TEETH RATTLE

Why is it always arresting--
the sight of that same metal-sharp
disc of moon slicing slick and clean
as if it spun on a motor through
purple autumn clouds?

Likewise, I'm startled, taken aback
this morning, by three long-tailed
weasels humping cattywampus across
the gravel road, disappearing
into the weed-tunnels of oxeye daisy
and dock in the roadside ditches.

There's a whole prairie of popped
yucca pods, an overdone, unrestrained
confetti-spilling deluge of seeds
that's stopped me before, and I admit
I've stared--a tribe of darkling beetles
on the path, all standing on their heads,
black rear-ends to the wind. Like this,
like this, like this.

Whoever said *the ordinary, the mundane,*
the commonplace? Show them to me.

Wait a minute--a hummingbird moth
so deep now inside a rose petunia
that its petals flutter too, like wings.

There's no remedy, I suppose—this body
just made from the beginning to be shocked,
constantly surprised, perpetually stunned,
poked and prodded, shaken awake,
shaken again and again roughly, rudely,
then left, even more bewildered,
even more amazed.

.   .   .   .   .

IN MY TIME

It's easy to praise things present--the belligerent
stance of the woodhouse toad, the total
self-absorption of the frostweed blossom.
It's simple to compliment a familiar mess
of curly dock, the serene organization
of common onion reeds, the radish bulb
and its slender purple tail. And I like the way
the jay flings dirt furiously this morning
from the window box, the ridiculous shakings
of his black beak.

But it's not easy to praise things yet-to-come--
the nonexistent nubs of mountains not risen
from beneath the floor of the sea
or a new sound from some new creature,
descended maybe from our golden peepers
and white-chinned chuggers, that sound
becoming synonymous, for someone else,
with spring.

How can I appreciate light from an aging
sun shining through new configurations neither pine
nor ash? How can I extol the nurturing
fragrances from the spires, the spicules
of a landscape not yet formed or seeded?

I can praise these flowers today—the white yucca
with its immersing powder-covered moth, the desert
tahoka daisy and the buffalo gourd—but never
the future strangeness that may eventually
take their places.

From here now, I simply praise in advance
the one who will be there then,
so moved, as I, to do the praising.

. . . . .

IF DYING MEANS BECOMING PURE SPIRIT

Then I think it must be like falling,
that giving-up of the body.
Who wouldn't try to catch hold
of something fast, jerk forward, reaching
with the fingers spread, before the hands
were gone, before the arms
disappeared?

I could never willingly withdraw
from my ribs, pull out of the good bars
and cage, leave the marrow, the temple
of salt, of welling and subsiding, abandon
complacently the swallow, the tongue, the voice.

How could I regard a crab apple
flustered with long-stalked blossoms
or a sycamore hung with nutlets and tufts,
with no face to catch the shadow-splatter
of their limbs and leaves? How could I apprehend
mixed fields of cordgrasses and barleys,
with no breath to detect the scent
of their sedges and clefts?

Even though it's said the spirit
is weightless, still, I think it must be
like falling a terrible fall,
to leave the body, to speed away
backwards, cut off from the humming
a cappella of pines, the skeltered
burring of grasshoppers, from the fragrances
of low wood fires beside a river, clean
ice on stalks of cattail and rye, lost
to the purple spice of scattered
thunders, no belly left to feel
the wide, easy range of the earth.

I admit to being angry
and frightened tonight at the thought
of such a plummeting.

THE LAYING ON OF HANDS

There's a gentleness we haven't learned yet,
but we've seen it--the way an early morning haze
can settle in the wayside hedges of lilac and yew,
permeate the emptiness between every scaly
bud and leafstalk until it becomes bound,
fully contained, shaped by the spires,
the stiff pins and purple-white blossoms
of that tangled wall.

There's a subtlety we haven't mastered yet,
but we recognize it--the way moonlight passes
simultaneously upon, through, beyond
the open wing of the crane fly
without altering a single detail
of its smallest paper vein. We know
there is a perfect consideration
of touching possible. The merest snow
accomplishes that, assuming the exact
configuration of the bristled beggarweed
while the beggarweed remains
exclusively itself.

If I could discover that same tension
of muscle myself, if I could move, imagining
smoke finding the forest-lines of the sun
at dusk, if I could place my hand
with that motion, achieve the proper
stance of union and isolation
in fingers and palm, place my hand
with less pressure than a water strider
places by the seeds of its toes
on the surface of the pond, balance
that way, skin to bark, my hand
fully open on the trunk of this elm tree

right now, I know it would be possible
to feel immediately every tissue imposition
and ringed liturgy, every bloodvein
and vacuum of that tree's presence, perceive
immediately both the hard, jerking start
of the seedling in winter and the spore-filled
moss and liquid decay of the fallen trunk
to come, both the angle of tilt in the green sun
off every leaf above and the slow lightning
of hair roots in their buried dark below,
know even the reverse silhouette of my own hand
experienced from inner bark out,
even the moment of this very revelation
of *woman and tree* itself where it was locked
millennia before in those tight molecules
of suckers and sapwood.

Without harm or alteration or surrender
of any kind, I know my hand laid properly,
could discover this much.

. . . . .

EATING DEATH

Suppose I had never distinguished myself
to myself from the landscape
so that reaching out to touch a leaf
of chickasaw plum or a spiny pondweed
underwater were no different to me
from putting my hand on my knee or pulling
my fingers through my hair.

And that which was not tangible
I understood as my expression to myself
of my inclinations--my violet serenity

synonymous with distant levels of blue
rain against a ruddy hill, my opening circling
into sex identical with the gold and russet
revolution of the sun into dusk.

In the new forming of lilac
or pear blossoms I realized the color
and fragrance of my balance redefined
every spring. I knew the horizon
as that seam made by the meeting
of my sight and my word, and recognized
the night and the day as my own slow
breathing in and slow breathing out
of light.

Then surely the small ebony hobble
I'd notice one evening appearing
out of an ancient canyon syntax, I'd understand
simply as a further aspect of myself.
And as it became larger, slowly obliterating
the purpose and combustible prairie-presence
of myself, I wouldn't be frightened, knowing
that it came to me from my own depths,
its empty eyes my creation, its steady
grin the white stone of my history.
And when it lifted and spread
its cloak finally, as if it were my will
filling the sky, and I called it my name,
it would be easy to be taken and covered
by my own possession, to put my mouth
against it, my star-pocked arms tight
around its neck, to draw in, sucking,
swallowing, consuming completely
every quiet fold and release
of the last event of my life.

FOREPLAY

When it first begins, as you might expect,
the lips and thin folds are closed, the pouting
layers pressed, lapped lightly,
almost languidly, against one another
in a sealed bud.

However, with certain prolonged
and random strokings of care
along each binding line, with soft
intrusions traced beneath each pursed
gathering and edge, with inquiring
intensities of gesture—as the sun
swinging slowly from winter back
to spring, touches briefly,
between moments of moon and masking
clouds, certain stunning points
and inner nubs of earth—so
with such ministrations, a slight
swelling, a quiver of reaching,
a tendency toward space,
might be noticed to commence.

Then with dampness from the dark,
with moisture from the falling
night of morning, from hidden places
within the hills, each seal begins
to loosen, each recalcitrant clasp
sinks away into itself, and every tucked
grasp, every silk tack willingly relents,
releases, gives way, proclaims a turning,
declares a revolution, assumes,
in plain sight, a surging position

that offers, an audacious offering
that beseeches, every petal parted wide.

Remember the spiraling, blue
valerian, remember the violet, sucking
larkspur, the laurel and rosebay
and pea cockle flung backwards, remember
the fragrant, funneling lily, the lifted
honeysuckle, the sweet, open pucker
of the ground ivy blossom?

Now even the darkest crease possessed,
the most guarded, pulsing, least drop
of pearl bead, moon grain trembling
deep within is fully revealed, fully exposed
to any penetrating wind or shaking fur
or mad hunger or searing, plunging surprise
the wild descending sky in delirium
has to offer.

. . . . .

ARE SOME SINS HOSANNAS?

Those sins, for example, of amplitude,
of over-abundance, like the unrestrained
seeding of the blue yucca, the mink frog
and dusky crawfish frog, the spore-gorged
tumbling puffball? You've seen this transgression
in the cottonwood too, covering the river,
burdening the summer with more drifting,
white fluff and flurry than anyone
ever requested, replicating over and over
and over, as if being were worth it.

Are certain sins, of arrogance for instance,
a form of praise, the way the mullein
and the vinegar weed shoot straight up
from the earth unabashed, taking
overmuch pride in their stances, pointing
their flower-covered batons toward the sky
as if they were a righteousness?
This is the same haughty act the stalks
of sotol and steeplebush, the audacious
lodgepole pine and towering lousewort perform.

Is the noise of too much joy a madness
condemned by more moderate gods
who surely know better? Hush, hush
chortling heathen toads, unredeemed, triple-
chirping field crickets, ceaseless
sinning *tsee* of waxwings, spring-forest
sweet-sweet-sweet of wood warblers.

If some sins are truly jubilations,
then with you here beside me again
tonight, I'm certain I offend
many gods myself. I confess it and repent,
repent with the most contrite
voice I can manage, pulling my pillow
over my face, lying on my hands to try
to stop this rude sacrilege, my uncontrollable
crooning of happiness, incessant caressing,
touching your body everywhere, a sliding
vine of butterfly pea openly curling,
binding, such decadent opulence, my long,
excessive murmurs of immeasurable
adoration.

FETAL BAT: THE CREATION
OF THE VOID

Tender in its absolute predestination—four
long, deformed finger bones, plum-round
body, umbrella wings—it's an inevitability
begun by bat penis, sperm dart, bat
ovum, bat pocket of womb where it flutters,
flickers sporadically, warm and drowned
in swaying pearl-clear waters.

The fetus folds in its place, tightens,
settles again, shoulder-hunched knuckles
drawn to its ears, a vestigial claw
to its chin. Its eyes are thinly lidded.
Its tongue, slender, pliable as a single
leaflet of summer fern, moves back
slightly in its throat as if to suckle.

A pea-sized heart swings inside
the tiny night of its chest inside the night
behind its mother's teats and blue
coming-milk inside the still stone cavern
of night where she hangs by one foot upside
down inside the universe of night
with its shifting, combusting summary
of stars wheeling inside, outside.

When this fetus emerges,
feet first, born alive, clinging
to its mother's breast, legs curled
beneath her armpit, drying the fine fuzz
of its face and features, the translucent
dun and veined-scarlet silk skin
of its wings stretched wide, it screams,

screeches wildly, setting every petal
of yucca and sweet chicory that blooms
inside its rare garden to shivering,
to ringing.

What a very first phenomenon
it makes as it occupies so perfectly
such a definite empty space, the only void
of itself which we recognize now
never anywhere, until this moment
of its birth, existed at all.

.   .   .   .   .

INFANTICIDE

Sometimes they were put in baskets, little nests
of rushes and leaves. (Someone had to weave
these water-cradles for them--the threading
fingers of grandmother, auntie, midwife.)
They were placed in their casket-boats
and launched, and if they couldn't swim,
whose fault was that?

Some were curled, heads touching knees,
in their womb positions inside clay jars,
then set along temple porticoes
in case some passing worshipper might want
a baby for a slave. Their fretting
voices in the corridors were as common
and hoarse as dry cicadas, till they died.

Some were burned for expiation to the gods,
in ceremonies, shrill trumpets and cymbals
covering their cries. Some were placed naked,

still bloody, on icy pinnacles in dark snow.
Some were strangled, some tortured
to death, some eaten, a few hours old.
After all, nobody knew them yet.

Some were flung off canyon cliffs,
even on a spring afternoon, the prairie
colored with clover and milkvetch,
or even on a damp autumn morning,
the plums red and sweet and fragrant.

Mary Hamilton bore her baby alone
in the King's forest, leaning back, pressing
against an oak, her skirts pulled up,
and all the while watching the patterns
above her, layered leaves, sky pieces,
branches and boughs constricting, widening
with the wind. Then she killed him with a knife.

Gone, murdered by deliberate
acts--I don't think anyone
ever counted them all--those cursed, born
during lightning storms or under a bad
moon or feetfirst or blind, born
during war or a hard journey, into starvation,
those with the wrong fathers, the girls,
the unwanted. It was the custom,
and there were reasons, burdens.
Even mothers said so.

From every stone-cut or gnawed
umbilical, from every bud-sized
fist, every thumb and finger petal
folded inward, from every perfectly
stitched violet thread, every temple pulse,
every rib shudder of this elegy,
relieve us.

GODDAMN THEOLOGY

It was easier when you were a jonquil
and I was a fingertip pressed at the juncture
of your radiating petals and stiff stem.
And it was not so difficult
when I was a Persian guitar
and you were the knee on which I lay,
my neck held easily in your hand.

But there were problems
when you were two hundred years of years,
twisted like taffy, twisted and looped
like a dry bristlecone in dusty snow,
and I was just a beginning sliver
of clear, tadpole breath in a whorl
of waterweed. I didn't know
what to say.

And when I thought I knew your name,
and I called it out loud many times,
that's when you were a deaf sheaf
of catacombed coral with more
than one title and no tongue.

I was whole, a burning ball of peach
hanging from a branch. You were multiple,
sparks struck from a hammer against rock.
I split into a showering orbit of mayflies
in the evening sun. You congealed
into a seeded cow patty in the field.

When the painted pony and I were galloping
fast through rabid waves on the beach,
there you were, a tiny spire of ship
sailing off the edge of the sea.

The night I woke in white, my body moon-grey,
you were curled, a black hump of quilt
at the foot of my bed, dead asleep.

And later when you were falling rapidly,
heavily, raindrops and pockdrops and bullet
marks, a mob in the mountain lake, I was precise
wing and talon over the prairie, jackknifing
and stabbing, lifting the mouse by her spine.

When I was crying, crying and truly
sorry, you were a spray of chartreuse
and scarlet tinfoil confetti on my head.

That's when I knew for certain
it was going to be much more difficult
than we'd ever imagined before.

. . . . .

LIFE IN AN EXPANDING UNIVERSE

It's not only all those cosmic
pinwheels with their charging solar
luminosities, the way they spin around
like the paper kind tacked to a tree trunk,
the way they expel matter and light
like fields of dandelions throwing off
waves of summer sparks in the wind,
the way they speed outward,
receding, creating new distances
simply by soaring into them.

But it's also how the noisy
crow enlarges the territory

above the landscape at dawn, making
new multiple canyon spires in the sky
by the sharp towers and ledges
of its calling; and how the bighorn
expand the alpine meadows by repeating
inside their watching eyes every foil
of columbine and bell rue, all
the stretches of sedges, the candescences
of jagged slopes and crevices existing there.

And though there isn't a method
to measure it yet, by finding
a golden-banded skipper on a buttonbush,
by seeing a blue whiptail streak
through desert scrub, by looking up
one night and imagining the fleeing
motions of the stars themselves, I know
my presence must swell one flutter-width
wider, accelerate one lizard-slip farther,
descend many stellar-fathoms deeper
than it ever was before.

.   .   .   .   .

CREATING TRANSFIGURATION

It only took staying still, standing
in the right place at the right time, arms
held out sideways straight from the body,
standing still like that on the shore, the winter
wind blowing ice-fog and freezing spray
in from the sea in swelling shrouds
and moanings all night;

to stand there, ice slowly shelling
the body in smooth white glass,

forming, hour by hour, thick glistening
pillars around bone, frost tassels
of tangled hair, clear, solid ribbons
of sea frozen in fringe hanging down
from the fingers and chin, furrowing
like tears stopped on the cheeks;

only to stand still letting the stinging
sea-drizzle fasten to face and breast
in the dark, form choirs of ice on spine,
ribs, knuckles, name; to stay at dawn,
staring unmoved toward the horizon, crystal
body gold in the sun, steam rising
like a holy spirit of light in the sun;

then to let them all, waking, come,
some running, some on knees, some bringing
candles in paper cups, peaches dried
with clove, some carrying violet lilies
and spindled whelks, others placing markers,
smooth stones, like loaves of bread, piled
in cairns on the sand for signs, all
circling round and round, all imbued
and radiant, all promising,
all transfigured.

. . . . .

FOR ANY KNOWN FACT:
NUDE WALKING ALONE ON
A BEACH IN MOONLIGHT

One might easily become confused
about proper designations. The beach
is as white, as tense and dedicated

as the moon, it could be stated.
Or should one say the moon presses
through the black sky as steady, reflective
and waxen as a nude body sequined
with spray walks through the night?

The sound of such convoluted thinking
has the same sound as the surf, perhaps;
for the speaking surf has many tongues
that divulge and stutter, prod forward
fondling, withdrawing.

The black sea surface glitters
with bobbing, stuttering moons as flat
as light. Likewise the black body
of any single fish is covered
with thousands of glassy moons, and each drop
of spray on a nude body—jewelling the neck,
beading the lashes, tresses and ear tips,
sparkling down the ivory legs—becomes moon
and mirror simultaneously.

Along the beach of the one distant,
completely naked moon, a strolling figure
might be detected. The moon is a mirror,
surely, but is a mirror a forbidden window
becoming itself by its own reflective act,
or is it just a dull word of unenlightened
imitation?

To turn and walk deliberately out
into the convoluted surf, to feel
the dedicated sounds of that surf
rising gradually to cover the thighs,
the breasts, the eyes, to say the sinking
lungs are filled with waves of fondling

moons, the heart stopped with silent
salt-light—it could be called *suicide,*
but that's just a single word, a thrashing
sound covered with reflective scales,
a stuttering word that might mean to see
suddenly, in this black and alabaster
world, an orange-violet reflection
in a transfigured window, a startling
scarlet-blue sphere of body
and image as one, or it might mean
merely to watch, without interfering,
as that barely recognizable figure
of white light unclothed in the mirror
steps precisely and manifestly off
the edge of the moon.

.   .   .   .   .

THE IMAGE IN A WORLD
OF FLUX

As black as tropic heat on a windowless
night, black as the center of poison, black
as the scorched edges of an old prayer, the cat
sits upright, tail curled around her paws.

She's the only consistent being here
for as far as anyone can see, surrounded
as she is by shooting and sinking pellets
of plains, by fields that startle in rattles
and coughs, rivers that mend in curtsies,
relinquish in spells, reclaim
in gales and graveyards.

Yet she sits, a composition of bone
and bevy, throat strumming, satiated,
oriental, dozing. Her reflection on the sky
in the swarmy sea is split open and sealed
constantly, copped and bound, snatched
in hooks of salt, rocked by pistons
and wheels of water, fang and whisker
drawn under, yawning and licking lifted up.

Her reflection rests serene in puzzled
fragments on the glass dome smashed
and glued together again and again.

As still as a marble saint in a vault,
as stopped as *12:00 midnight* spoken aloud,
she's the measuring rod, the magnetic pole,
the spine, the axis around which the rackets
of the surf strike, ameliorate, reverse
themselves, define their exploding equations,
deny their names in fog and ice. She's the base
tagged and abandoned repeatedly.

Watch out. Watch out. There's a sudden
conflagration. A flame catches hold
at the corner of this picture beginning
to crisp and curl under, smoke and ashes moving
rapidly in a diagonal across the world
toward my fingers.

But see, she's leaping, leaping,
white now, invisible, up and out, escaping
to clutch a bare branch as real and definite
as this network of black cracks we see spread
in its steady place across the blank,
blank ceiling over our heads.

THE ALL-ENCOMPASSING
Philosopher in Meditation,

BY REMBRANDT

The philosopher is the old, bearded
man in the red beanie, dozing,
it seems, in the sun by the window.
Before him on the table lies his ponderous
volume open to the indirect
light of the day.

But the philosopher could be
the bent firekeeper by the wall
behind the stairs. He stirs, rouses
the coals, studies the combustion.
He's hunched and crotchety there,
concentrating obviously as he constructs
his viable conflagration.

The solid spiral, helix staircase,
curving down the middle of the room,
could be the philosophy, each step leading
naturally and logically to the next.
It's the physical form of ordered thought
reaching a grand staircase conclusion.
The carpenter, then, is the missing seer.

Yet the small round door (dwarf-size)
behind the old man, rightly accepts,
by portal philosophy, that it must meditate
on its closed and locked condition
until a key appears, at which time
it must assimilate the revelation of *open.*

Does the blind black in the corners
beyond the reach of the window radiance,

as well as the cavern maw at the top
curve of the stairs, match the oblivion
in the sleep of the thinker? If so,
then the sun works a philosophy itself
by realizing the window ledge, the pottery
on the sill and idle book, the folded hands,
the dropped chin. And the old scholar
sleeps in the light of the known.

O philosopher's meditation, don't you understand,
even the baskets and barrels and pots
and smoke of this hovel that split
and bang and cling, and the firekeeper
cracking his throat and the bucket
of ashes and clinkers on the hearth,
and each separate meditation in its place
and time, all these must take their positions
in the rhetoric of the system?

If I hear the ancient housewife rattling
and creaking now down the curve of the stairs
(old gene, spiral of conception, old twist),
dogs scrambling at her heels, broom
and dustpan knocking, if she enters here
with her raucous retinue, cursing and barking,
jolts the sleeper, sweeping under the old man's
stool, cuffs the firekeeper, sets the pans
and spoons swinging, then all previous
suppositions fail, and we must begin again.

EATING BREAD AND HONEY (1997)

THE SINGING PLACE

For the orange, saucer-eyed
lemurs indri of the family sifaka,
it is the perfect forest of the hot,
humid zones. There, at sunset and dawn,
they all pause arboreally and chorus,
howling, hooting, shaking the shadows
overhead, the fruits and burrowing
beetles inside the many-storied
jungle. They are the ushers,
the chaperones, the screaming
broadcast of darkness and light.

The house cricket, the field cricket,
the dead-leaf cricket make song places
of the warmest, darkest niches
they can find, at the bases of stones,
in grass stem funnels, the mossy
underbark of southside tree trunks.

For the sage grouse, male, the real
singing place is where he actually sings,
there inside the thimble-sized, flesh-
and-blood place of his voice, that air
sac burbling and popping, puffing

through the morning as he struts
and bows before his hens on the open
spring lek. Breath, I believe,
is place.

And maybe even the bulb and tuber
and root suck of the big black slug
of wet pastures could be called a long,
slow mud music and meter of sustenance,
by those lucky enough to be born
with a pasture sense for sound.

The whine and wind of heat
through ragged gorges make sandstone
and basalt a moving song. And place,
I think, is moments in motion.

As on the white-statue plains
of the moon's most weird winter
where no dusk scream or lingering suck
or floosing air sac of song has ever
existed, utter stillness is a singing
place too, moments where I first
must find a shape of silence,
where I then must begin
to hum its structure.

. . . . .

OPUS FROM SPACE

Almost everything I know is glad
to be born--not only the desert orangetip,
on the twist flower or tansy, shaking
birth moisture from its wings, but also the naked
warbler nestling, head wavering toward sky,

and the honey possum, the pygmy possum,
blind, hairless thimbles of forward,
press and part.

Almost everything I've seen pushes
toward the place of that state as if there were
no knowing any other—the violent crack
and seed-propelling shot of the witch hazel pod,
the philosophy implicit in the inside out
seed-thrust of the wood sorrel. All hairy
salt cedar seeds are single-minded
in their grasping of wind and spinning
for luck toward birth by water.

And I'm fairly shocked to consider
all the bludgeonings and batterings going on
continually, the head-rammings, wing-furors,
and beak-crackings fighting for release
inside gelatinous shells, leather shells,
calcium shells or rough, horny shells. Legs
and shoulders, knees and elbows flail likewise
against their womb walls everywhere, in pine
forest niches, seepage banks and boggy
prairies, among savannah grasses, on woven
mats and perfumed linen sheets.

Mad zealots, every one, even before
beginning they are dark dust-congealings
of pure frenzy to come into light.

Almost everything I know rages to be born,
the obsession founding itself explicitly
in the coming bone harps and ladders,
the heart-thrusts, vessels and voices
of all those speeding with clear and total
fury toward this singular honor.

THE FALLACY OF THINKING
FLESH IS FLESH

Some part of every living creature
is always trembling, a curious
constancy in the wavering rims
of the cup coral, the tasseling
of fringe fish, in the polyrippling
of the polyclad flatworm even under the black
bottom water at midnight when nothing
in particular notices.

The single topknot, head feather,
of the horned screamer or the tufted
quail can never, in all its tethered
barbs and furs, be totally still.
And notice the plural flickers
of the puss moth's powdery antennae.
Not even the puss moth knows how
to stop them.

Maybe it's the pattern of the shattering
sea-moon so inherent to each body
that makes each more than merely body.
Maybe it's the way the blood possesses
the pitch and fall of blooming grasses
in a wind that makes the prairie
of the heart greater than its boundaries.
Maybe it's god's breath swelling
in the breast and limbs, like a sky
at dawn, that gives bright bone
the holiness of a rising sun.
There's more to flesh than flesh.

The steady flex and draw of the digger
wasp's blue-bulbed abdomen—I know

there's a fact beyond presence
in all that fidgeting.

Even as it sleeps, watch the body
perplex its definition—the slight shift
of the spine, the inevitable lash shiver,
signal pulse knocking. See, there,
that simple shimmer of the smallest
toe again, just to prove it.

. . . . .

MURDER IN THE GOOD LAND

Murder among the creek narrows
and shafts of rice grass, among lacy
coverlets and field sacks, among basement
apple barrels and cellar staples
of onion and beet;
                          beneath piled stones,
razed, broken and scattered stones,
beneath cow bridges, draw bridges, T girders
crossed, and cables, beneath brome, spadefoot,
beneath roots of three-awn
                          and heaven; murder
in the sky between stalks of spikesedge,
between harrier and wolf willow, between
the bedroom walls of formidable sluts
and saints, in the sad blindnesses
of moon and mole, in light as curt
and clearcut as blades of frost
magnified;
                    through blanks of winter wind
through summer soapweed, through welcoming
gates and bolted gates, throughout the blood-rushing
grief of the swarmy sea;

                            murder beside gods
down heathen colonnades, down corridors of scholars
and beggars, down the cathedral colonnades
of orchards in harvest;
                            murder with the clench
of white clover, with the slip of the wandering
tattler, with the slow splash of window
curtains flowing inward
                            with morning air; murder
in the winsome, murder in the wayward,
murder in canyon wrens, in the low beating bell
in the womb, in bone rafters,
                            in mushroom
rings and rosy rings; murder, murder,
murder immortal, pervasive, supreme
everywhere in the good land.

.   .   .   .   .

NEARING AUTOBIOGRAPHY

Those are my bones rifted
and curled, knees to chin,
among the rocks on the beach,
my hands splayed beneath my skull
in the mud. Those are my rib
bones resting like white sticks
wracked on the bank, laid down,
delivered, rubbed clean
by river and snow.

Ethereal as seedless weeds
in dim sun and frost, I see
my own bones translucent as locust
husks, light as spider bones,
as filled with light as lantern

bones when the candle flames.
And I see my bones, facile,
willing, rolling and clacking,
reveling like broken shells
among themselves in a tumbling surf.

I recognize them, no other's,
raggedly patterned and wrought,
peeled as a skeleton of sycamore
against gray skies, stiff as a fallen
spruce. I watch them floating
at night, identical lake slivers
flush against the same star bones
drifting in scattered pieces above.

Everything I assemble, all
the constructions I have rendered
are the metal and dust of my locked
and storied bones. My bald cranium
shines blind as the moon.

.   .   .   .   .

OF POSSIBILITY: ANOTHER AUTUMN LEAVING

Here they come like miniature herds
of headless ponies without hooves,
stampeding, rearing, trampling one another.
They corral to circle upward themselves
like air-borne droves of crippled brown
crows, rising in fragments of dust spouts,
raining down singly in swiveling pieces.

As if they were blind, they batter
against barricades, pile along brick

walls, boulders, wooden fences, filling
gullies and clefts, multitudes deep
as if they had no need to breathe.
Even with bodies without lungs,
there's a ghost cusp and sigh, a hollow
desert buzz to their rousing.

They sweep all night in the dry-moon
rasp of their rattling trance.
They scutter and reel up the windowpanes
on their hundred pins, over the roof
in their thorny flocks. Though totally
lacking bones or the tatters of bones,
still they shrivel and quake.
Though totally devoid of hearts
or the rubbish of hearts, still
they are brittle and heedless.

Even without souls, they shiver and rend.
Even without devils, they make ritual
processions of their deprivations. With no
word at all, they lie. They stutter.
They testify to themselves. Even lost
and without a god, they make visions
of the invisible, become the buffet,
the possessed, the very place of wind.
They are the time and tangible nexus
of all heavenly spirits. Even without tongues,
they clatter their tongues.

CREATION BY THE PRESENCE OF ABSENCE: CITY COYOTE IN RAIN

She's sleek blue neon through
the blue of the evening. She's black
sheen off the blue of wet streets,
blue daunt of suspension in each
pendant of rain filling the poplars
on the esplanade.

Her blue flank flashes once in the panes
of empty windows as she passes.
She's faster than lighthouse blue
sweeping the seas in circles.

Like the leaping blue of flames
burning in an alley barrel, her presence
isn't perceived until she's gone.

She cries with fat blue yelps, calls
with the scaling calls of the ragmen,
screeches a siren of howls along the docks
below the bridges, wails with the punctuated
griefs of drunks and orphans.

She scuttles under gates, through doors
hanging by broken hinges, behind ash
bins, into a culvert, shakes off the storm
in an explosion of radiance, licks
the cold muzzles and genitals of her frenzied
pups, gives them her blue teats, closes
her yellow eyes.

No one ever sees her face to face,
or those who do never know they do,

denying her first, pre-empting her lest
the place of pattern and time she creates,
like the blue of a star long since
disintegrated, enter their hearts
with all of its implications.

. . . . .

THE DEATH OF LIVING ROCKS AND THE CONSEQUENCES THEREOF

The god of rocks said *stop,*
and all the rocks stopped still
where they were--wolf rocks, pouncing
or suckling, packed in the forest,
snake rocks singling over the desert,
rock toads, their round pebbly
humps huddled along streambeds.

They all stopped--whale boulders
impassive on the floor of the sea, seal
rocks piled shiny and herded in spray
on the shore, a rock puma, granite
teeth bared, her rock kittens scattered
and halted half way down the hill,
closed mica butterfly wings.

Whole swaths of gypsum stems
and flowerets became paralysed
where we see them now, unmoved
in the wind. Pipes of organ rocks
and the red bugle rocks beside them
posed statuesque over ravines
and gulches without music.

On the day the god of rocks
said *stop,* all the rocks of the earth
stood still, without further expression,
without further response. And the god
of rocks, simply a possible reflection
of his own rock creation, became bound himself,
eyes staring marble white, voice a solid
layer of shale, the words *live again*
soundless and locked irretrievably
on his silent, stone tongue.

. . . . .

THE CONSEQUENCES OF DEATH

You might previously have thought
each death just a single loss.
But when a plain gray titmouse dies,
what plunges simultaneously and disappears too
are all the oak-juniper woodlands,
the streamside cottonwoods, every elderberry
bush and high spring growth of sprouted
oak once held inside its eye.

And when a sugar pine splits, breaks
to the ground, falling with its fiestas
and commemorations of blue-green needles,
long-winged seeds, the sweet resin
of its heartwood, there's another
collapse coincident--a fast inward
sinking and sucking back to nothing
of all those stars once kept in its core,
those clusters of suns and shining
dusts once resident in the sky of its rigid

bark and cone-scales. We could hear
the sound of that galactic collapse as well,
if we had the proper ears for it.

And when a mountain sheep stumbles,
plummmets, catapulting skull, spine,
from cliffside to crumbling rock below,
a like shape of flame and intensity
on a similar sharp ledge on the other side
of the same moment, out of our sense,
loses balance, goes blind.

Because of these torn paper-shreds
of gold-lashed wings, this spangled
fritillary's death, somewhere behind the night
a convinced declaration of air and matter
and intention, silenced, speaks no longer
of the god of its structure.

.   .   .   .   .

AGAINST THE ETHEREAL

I'm certain these are the only angels
there are: those with raised, sneering
lips revealing razor-pure incisors that rip
with a purpose, dominions in the moment
when they spread like flying squirrels,
sail like jaguarundi across the celestials
with sickle claws thrust forward.

This is the only rite of holiness
I know: fierce barb of bacteria, that hot,
hot coal, that smoldering challenge

glaring, for twelve millennia at least,
in all directions from its dark, sub-zero
cellar of frozen, glacial rock.

This is the noise of heavenly
hosts: trumpet-blaring chaparrals
and shinneries, cymbal-banging greasewood
and jojoba deserts, burble of hellbinders, slips
of heliotropes, tweakings of brush mice
and big-eared bats, wheezings of rusty wheels,
grasshopper sparrows, autumn leaves ticking
across gravel on their paper pricks.

I aspire devotedly and with all reverence
to the raspy links of lampreys, the tight
latchings of pawpaw apples and soursops,
the perfect piercings and fastenings
of sperms and ovipositors, clinging
grasps of titis and chacmas.

Aren't you peculiarly frightened, as I am,
by the vague, the lax, the gossamer
and faint, the insubstantial and all
submissive, bowing transparencies,
any willfully pale worshipping?

This is the only stinging, magenta-cruel,
fire-green huffing, bellowing mayhemic
spirituality I will ever recognize:
the one shuddering with veined lightning,
chackling with seeded consolations, howling
with winter pities, posturing with speared
and fisted indignations, surly as rock, rude
as weeds, riotous as billbugs, tumultuous

as grapevine beetles, as large black, burying
beetles, bare, uncovered to every perception
of god, and never, never once forgiving
death.

. . . . .

ANIMALS AND PEOPLE: "THE HUMAN HEART IN CONFLICT WITH ITSELF"

Some of us like to photograph them. Some
of us like to paint pictures of them. Some of us
like to sculpt them and make statues and carvings
of them. Some of us like to compose music
about them and sing about them. And some of us
like to write about them.

Some of us like to go out
and catch them and kill them and eat them. Some
of us like to hunt them and shoot them and eat them.
Some of us like to raise them, care for them and eat
them. Some of us just like to eat them.

And some of us
name them and name their seasons and name their hours,
and some of us, in our curiosity, open them up
and study them with our tools and name their parts.
We capture them, mark them and release them,
and then we track them and spy on them and enter
their lives and affect their lives and abandon
their lives. We breed them and manipulate them
and alter them. Some of us experiment
upon them.

We put them on tethers and leashes,
in shackles and harnesses, in cages and boxes,
inside fences and walls. We put them in yokes
and muzzles. We want them to carry us and pull us
and haul for us.

And we want some of them
to be our companions, some of them to ride on our fingers
and some to ride sitting on our wrists or on our shoulders
and some to ride in our arms, ride clutching our necks.
We want them to walk at our heels.

We want them to trust
us and come to us, take our offerings, eat from our hands.
We want to participate in their beauty. We want to assume
their beauty and so possess them. We want to be kind
to them and so possess them with our kindness and so
partake of their beauty in that way.

And we want them
to learn our language. We try to teach them our language.
We speak to them. We put *our* words in *their* mouths.
We want *them* to speak. We want to know what they see
when they look at us.

We use their heads and their bladders
for balls, their guts and their hides and their bones
to make music. We skin them and wear them for coats,
their scalps for hats. We rob them, their milk
and their honey, their feathers and their eggs.
We make money from them.

We construct icons of them.
We make images of them and put their images on our clothes
and on our necklaces and rings and on our walls

and in our religious places. We preserve their dead
bodies and parts of their dead bodies and display
them in our homes and buildings.

                              We name mountains
and rivers and cities and streets and organizations
and gangs and causes after them. We name years and time
and constellations of stars after them. We make mascots
of them, naming our athletic teams after them. Sometimes
we name ourselves after them.

                              We make toys of them
and rhymes of them for our children. We mold them
and shape them and distort them to fit our myths
and our stories and our dramas. We like to dress up
like them and masquerade as them. We like to imitate them
and try to move as they move and make the sounds they make,
hoping, by these means, to enter and become the black
mysteries of their being.

                        Sometimes we dress them
in our clothes and teach them tricks and laugh at them
and marvel at them. And we make parades of them
and festivals of them. We want them to entertain us
and amaze us and frighten us and reassure us
and calm us and rescue us from boredom.

                              We pit them
against one another and watch them fight one another,
and we gamble on them. We want to compete with them
ourselves, challenging them, testing our wits and talents
against their wits and talents, in forests and on plains,
in the ring. We want to be able to run like them and leap
like them and swim like them and fly like them and fight
like them and endure like them.

                              We want their total
absorption in the moment. We want their unwavering devotion
to life. We want their oblivion.
                              Some of us give thanks
and bless those we kill and eat, and ask for pardon,
and this is beautiful as long as they are the ones dying
and we are the ones eating.

                     And as long as we are not
seriously threatened, as long as we and our children
aren't hungry and aren't cold, we say, with a certain
degree of superiority, that we are no better
than any of them, that any of them deserve to live
just as much as we do.

                     And after we have proclaimed
this thought, and by so doing subtly pointed out
that we are allowing them to live, we direct them
and manage them and herd them and train them and follow
them and map them and collect them and make specimens
of them and butcher them and move them here and move
them there and we place them on lists and we take
them off of lists and we stare at them and stare
at them and stare at them.

                     We track them in our sleep.
They become the form of our sleep. We dream of them.
We seek them with accusation. We seek them
with supplication.

                     And in the ultimate imposition,
as Thoreau said, we make them bear the burden
of our thoughts. We make them carry the burden
of our metaphors and the burden of our desires and our guilt
and carry the equal burden of our curiosity and concern.
We make them bear our sins and our prayers and our hopes

into the desert, into the sky, into the stars.
We say we kill them for God.
                              We adore them and we curse
them. We caress them and we ravish them. We want them
to acknowledge us and be with us. We want them to disappear
and be autonomous. We abhor their viciousness and lack
of pity, as we abhor our own viciousness and lack of pity.
We love them and we reproach them, just as we love
and reproach ourselves.

                    We will never, we cannot,
leave them alone, even the tiniest one, ever, because we know
we are one with them. Their blood is our blood. Their breath
is our breath, their beginning our beginning, their fate
our fate.

          Thus we deny them. Thus we yearn
for them. They are among us and within us and of us,
inextricably woven with the form and manner of our being,
with our understanding and our imaginations.
They are the grit and the salt and the lullaby
of our language.

                    We have a need to believe they are there,
and always will be, whether we witness them or not.
We need to know they are there, a vigorous life maintaining
itself without our presence, without our assistance,
without our attention. We need to know, we *must* know,
that we come from such stock so continuously and tenaciously
and religiously devoted to life.

                              We know we are one with them,
and we are frantic to understand how to actualize that union.
We attempt to actualize that union in our many stumbling,
ignorant and destructive ways, in our many confused
and noble and praiseworthy ways.

For how can we possess dignity
if we allow them no dignity? Who will recognize our beauty
if we do not revel in their beauty? How can we hope
to receive honor if we give no honor? How can we believe
in grace if we cannot bestow grace?

We want what we cannot
have. We want to give life at the same moment
we are taking it, nurture life at the same moment we light
the fire and raise the knife. We want to live, to provide,
and not be instruments of destruction, instruments
of death. We want to reconcile our "egoistic concerns"
with our "universal compassion." We want the lion
and the lamb to be one, the lion and the lamb
within finally to dwell together, to lie down together
in peace and praise at last.

. . . . .

THE ART OF RAISING GIBBONS
AND FLOWERS

We think they go well together--the translucent
vanilla orchid, the slipper orchid, the ginger
fragrances of the fiddle leaf, the swollen,
juice-filled buds of magnolia grandiflora,
Turkish tulip, Susa crocus, and the Siamang
gibbons who pound and scream, quarreling
and sweating, stinking inside their tight
cages where we have put them in the garden
under the iron oak trees.

They shake the bars, their snouts
dripping, piles of fecal matter covered
with green flies in the corners of their cages.

How they reek, puffing their red throat sacs
to holler and hoot in chorus at dawn and dusk.
The petals of the fringed iris and the tea-scented
China rose certainly shimmer then with that roar,
and even pollen spores and feeding butterflies
are shaken loose by the fetid blast.

But it all makes a nice contrast, we think.
So we allow the ranging wisteria to venture over
the east brick wall without pruning, the grape
hyachinths to spill supremely beyond the borders
of the walk. The spirea and trumpet vines
billow up through summer at will
like surf in a storm.

And the wide, white cups of gloriosa
blossoms hang down soft, confident
and abundant from the branches of the iron oak
where their vines have climbed. In an evening
breeze, we see them brush the roofs of those rank
cages, dawdle there in an evening breeze.
They sway and hush out of sight. Their perfume
and nectar-rain are dizzying. Their petals
shine with moonlight, just barely beyond
the reach of the horny black fingers stretching
through the bars to scratch, to encase.

Later we come close to the cages to watch
the gibbons sleeping, the straggly hairy
nakedness of their curled bodies. We imagine
they dream that the crusty callouses and bunyons
of their hands and feet have turned to camellias,
to petals of pale nolana, that they sip the liquor
of honeysuckle and drink the ices of violets
and orange blossoms. We imagine they dream
that their arms and torsos are supple

vines and sturdy trunks rising unrestrained
into the night, carrying moonlight
on the blossoms and graces of their bodies
up through the sky and back to the source
of that shining.

There's a certain pity and hope
made evident by this, which is the art
we carry with us like a penance out of the garden,
along the path, and down the darkened
hallways to our beds.

.   .   .   .   .

KISSING A KIT FOX

The kit fox has fine lips. Often black
or grey, they are as demure as two slight
fronds of Mayweed in fog, yet a little fuller.
They are capable of pulling back,
disappearing up and into the nether
to reveal his impressive fangs.

The lips of the kit fox taste
sometimes of the sweet spring water
he drank in its dark rock the moment before.
They taste also sometimes of the rank
bone marrow of the dead peccary
he licked in the ditch for a meal.
His lips and breath today tasted
of the peanut of dessicated
grasshoppers burned dry.

The needle teeth of the kit fox
when kissing sometimes pierce the lover's

tongue with sevenfold hot spears
like the sun. Often too they puncture
the lips of the lover and bring blood
to the mouth like the moon. A few cherish
this pain when kissing the kit fox,
because they believe they then may speak
with the authority of scars
on the nature of day and night.

And when kissing a kit fox,
some are lucky, for he will occasionally
wrap the thick ragrances of his plush
tail around the lover's neck up to the ears,
or better, across the eyes and over the nose.
One may then fall completely into the lush
swoon and smother of his race and art—cactus
juice, thorns and the musk of fear, snake
seed, fecal rat.

Some say kissing the kit fox
is a story, because it has both character
and event, both union and scorn.
But some say it is a song in syncopation
that they may tap to themselves
in loneliness for comfort. Others say kissing
the kit fox is a place one may enter,
a location with boundaries fixed in space,
a measurable site in a portion of time.
I say kissing a kit fox is like memory,
because it is a mere invention of pleasure
and pain, a creation of wild risk
with wound and fetish, certain evidence
of either the unlikely or the lost.

PLACE AND PROXIMITY

I'm surrounded by stars. They cover me
completely like an invisible silk veil
full of sequins. They touch me, one by one,
everywhere—hands, shoulders, lips,
ankle hollows, thigh reclusions.

Particular in their presence, like rain,
they come also in streams, in storms.
Careening, they define more precisely
than wind. They enter, cheekbone,
breastbone, spine, skull, moving out
and in and out, through like threads,
like weightless grains of beads
in their orbits and rotations,
their ritual passages.

They are the luminescence of blood
and circuit the body. They are showers
of fire filling the dark, myriad spaces
of porous bone. What can be nearer
to flesh than light?

And I swallow stars. I eat stars.
I breathe stars. I survive on stars.
They sound precisely, humming in my nose,
in my throat, on my tongue. *Stars, stars.*

They are above me suspended, drifting,
caught in the loom of the elm, similarly enmeshed
in my hair. They are below me straight down
in the deep. I am immersed in stars. I swim
through stars, their swells and currents.

I walk on stars. They are less,
they are more, even than water,
even than earth.

They come with immediacy. They are as bound
to me as history. No knife, no death
can part us.

. . . . .

ABUNDANCE AND SATISFACTION

1.

One butterfly is not enough. We need
many thousands of them, if only
for the effusion of the wayward-
swaying words they occasion––blue
and copper hairstreaks, sulphur
and cabbage whites, brimstones,
peacock fritillaries, tortoiseshell
emperors, skippers, meadow browns.
We need a multitude of butterflies
right on the tongue simply to be able
to speak with a varied six-pinned
poise and particularity.

But thousands of butterflies
are surfeit. We need just one
flitter to apprehend correctly
the will of aspen leaves, the lassitude
of lupine petals, the sleep
of a sleeping eyelid. To examine
adequately one set of finely leaded,

stained wings of violet translucence,
one single sucking proboscis (sap-
and-sugar-licking thread), to study
thoroughly just one powder scale, one
gold speck from one dusted butterfly
forewing would require at least
a millenium of attention to all melody,
phrase, gravity and horizon.

2.

And just the same, one moon is more
than sufficient, ample complexity
and bewilderment—single waning crescent,
waxing crescent, lone gibbous, one perfect,
solitary sickle and pearl, one map
of mountains and lava plains, Mare
Nectaris, Crater Tycho. And how could
anyone really hold more than one full
moon in one heart?

Yet one moon is not enough. We need
millions of moons, glossy porcelain
globes glowing as if from the inside out,
weaving among each other in the sky
like lanterns bobbing on a black river
sea-bound. Then we could study
moons and the traversings of moons
and the multiple meanings of the phases
of moons, and the eclipsing of moons
by one another. We need a new language
of moons containing all the syllables
of interacting rocks of light
so that we might fully understand,
at last, the phrase 'one heart
in many moons.'

And of gods, we need just one, one
for the grief of twenty snow geese
frozen by their feet in ice and dead
above winter water. Yet we need twenty-
times-twenty gods for all the reccuring
memories of twenty snow geese frozen
by their feet in sharp lake-water ice.

But a single god suffices
for the union of joys in one school
of invisible green-brown minnows
flocking over green-brown stones
in a clear spring, but three gods
are required to wind and unwind
the braided urging of spring--root,
blossom and spore. And we need
the one brother of gods for a fragged
plain, blizzard-split, battered
by tumbleweeds and wire fences,
and the one sister to mind
the million sparks and explosions
of gods on fire in a pine forest.

I want one god to be both scatter
and pillar, one to explain simultaneously
mercy and derision, yet a legion of gods
for the spools of confusion and design,
but one god alone to hold me by the waist,
to rumble and quake in my ear, to dance me
round and round, one couple with forty
gods in the heavenly background
with forty violins with one
immortal baton keeping time.

"GOD IS IN THE DETAILS," SAYS MATHEMATICIAN FREEMAN J. DYSON

This is why grandmother takes such tiny
stitches, one stitch for each dust mote
of moon on the Serengeti at night, and one half
one stitch for each salt-fetch of fog
following the geometries of eelgrasses
in fields along the beach.

And this is why she changes the brief threads
in her glass needle so often—metallic bronze
for the halo around the thrasher's eye,
ruby diaphanous for the antenna tips
of the May beetle, transparent silk
for dry-rain fragrances blowing
through burr sages before rain.

She inserts her needle
through the center of each elementary
particle, as if it were a circling sequin
of blue, loops it to its orbit, sewing thus,
again and again, the reckless sapphire sea,
a whipping flag of tall summer sky.

Sometimes she takes in her hands
two slight breaths of needles at once,
needles so thin they almost burn
her fingers like splinters of light.
She crochets with them around each microscopic
void, invents, thereby, an ice tapestry
of winter on the window, creates a lace
of peeper shrillings through flooded
sweet gale, secures a blank jot of sight

in the knitting of each red flea
of zooplankton skittering mid-lake.

God's most minute exuberance is founded
in the way she sews with needles
as assertive as the sun-sharp loblolly
that she sees with her eyes closed;
in the way she knots stitches
as interlocked as the cries of veery,
peewee, black-capped chickadee and jay
that she hears with her ears stopped;
in the way she whispers to her work,
recites to her work, spooling every least
designation of spicule shade, hay
spider and air trifid, every hue
and rising act of her own hands. *Try
to escape now,* it reads, *just try.*

· · · · ·

RAPTURE OF THE DEEP:
THE PATTERN OF
POSEIDON'S LOVE SONG

The blue ornata's spiderweb
body sidles and pulses among the turning
cilia wheels of the microscopic
rotifera tilting over the feathery
fans of the splendidum slowly extending
and withdrawing
                              their fondling tongues
inside the body of the summer solstice
where the sun with its ragged
radiances organizes transparent
butterflies and paper kites of light

into flocks of meadow-drifting
throughout the green sea surrounding
the design
                    of string worms palolo
floating in the gripping and releasing
event of their own tight coils
toward a reef of chitons pulled
from their rock bases by the violent
bite and suck of a spinning
squall
            curling themselves then
into their round coat-of-mail shells
as if they were each one made
by the sound of long O moaning
inside a sailor's ancient prayer
to Mater Cara
                        tumbled and tumbled
by the waves beneath which the frilled
shark a singular presence in a dimension
of lesser constellations suspended
mid-sea whips with a graceful pattern
of pitiful evil
                    toward a nebula
of cephalopods undulating
below an arrangement of rain
shattering the evening suddenly
out of the linear into the million
falling moments
                        of one moment
pebbling the open plain of the sea
through which plankton ascend
like a legion of flittering spirits
or the single body of a multiple
deity swallowing stinging salt pieces
of stars

              to the surface to bask
beneath the violet order
of the traveling moon touching
all points in the declaration of birth
to death
              to stone embodied by shoals
of glass-threaded cod fluctuating
in their progress like schools of storm
petrels creating descent and angle
from a totally flat sky playing
a layering of flight
                     shadows off the eyes
of soaring dolphins breaching
with the contrapuntal rhythm of a passage
from Bach as over and within
this universe
              the hand of an ecstatic
wind its fingers spread wide
with blessing moves in a seizure
of joy through every trembling spray
and pulse and skeleton forming
the reality of this whole
prolonged consumation

.   .   .   .   .

THE LONG MARRIAGE:
A TRANSLATION

In among the alder's highest black
branches making a complicated map
of depth and elevation against the dull
white sky, winter waxwings in a flock
settle, coming, going.

They depart, altering the design of cold
and season in the tree, return
in gatherings of six or seven, flying
in quick staccato against a largo
of motion relative to one another,
as if they weren't birds alone
but a constantly changing syntax
in a history of place and event.

Several sail together over the fallen
field with an expansion and contraction
of pattern that might sound like a wheezing
of wooden organ or bagpipe, were there sound
to vision. And eleven spiral up, angle
into the evening like eleven dead leaves
with stunted wings and no more purpose
nor will than to illustrate eleven
different motives of the wind at once.

Gliding to gully, to river brush, a wave
of them parts easily, rejoins in crossing
familiarities that might impress like lavender
and sage, were there fragrances
to involution and grace.

Back and forth in ragged unison
through the network of branches, penetrating
and teetering, they leave the dense
scaffolding like torn pieces of broken tree
and veer toward the east; they return
from the west to circle and descend
again into the bare limbs of the alder
back in its place once more. Swerving
and sinking through the light,
they are a hard statement of fact
ameliorating itself midair.

I know evening and alder and waxwings
to one another can never be fixed. No constant
coordinate ever contains them. The new amber
of the sky moves toward darkness. Branches
and birds change places continuously,
as if definition also possessed no certain
form heightening and fading. Night stars,
invisible behind the hour, are bright
in the imagination, silent
with shifting prophecy.

.   .   .   .   .

E G G

Perhaps the light inside this temple
is less than a small candle barely
burning beneath a violet shade,
an uncertain diffusion like a glow
of glacier at night without moon,
a presence like morning over a pale
field before dawn, dimmer than day
with no voice to declare it.

Were there ears to hear inside
these halls, then a constant connecting
like scales of organ chords played
in arpeggio by two hands might be heard
as the spine assembles itself, a sound
like the low pizzicato of a cello
as the first faint plicking
of pulse commences.

One could claim a belief in crosses
exists predestined in the pattern

of arteries forming their junctures
yet to appear.

Were a seer present she might say
the attention inside this temple
is like that of rock spurs suddenly
quaked and rebounded by lightning.

Were a shaman present inside
these translucent walls, he might say
the sentiment is like that in a random
meadow of columbine filled
with mountain air before rain.

And were a master in the making here,
he might claim the process witnessed
in the rising and joining of warm wax
cells and oils is god, the exquisite
weaving of salt ropes and red twines
is the presence of god.

Though not one single star
exists in the curved breadth
of this structure, yet the only possible
place where any star might be found
is inside the immeasurable horizon
of the thin-skulled cranium about to be.

Could it be a worship of any kind
beheld in this first absence moving
toward a possible breath of protest
and sacrament?

When the last latching occurs, bringing
the rude kick and the cry, then this temple
must fail, fall, shatter away altogether,
and the world, at once, begin anew.

A COVENANT OF SEASONS (1998)

GOD'S ONLY BEGOTTEN DAUGHTER

If furling scarves of fire, flying
orange ribbons of bonfire by a dark lakeside
are beautiful, then she is beautiful.
If blue shrouds of snow or the fragrances
of summer grass freshly cut at dusk are desired,
then she is passion.

If the spawning of salmon fighting
upstream is a drama of obsession,
she is tragedian; if the grouse
in their mating are antic and raucous,
she is jester, clown. If the dart out
and back of an eel in its coral
cave is circumspect,
then she is so.

A vessel, yes, she contains like a sea,
like a scroll, like a crystal its pattern,
secure, symmetrical as honeycomb, woven
like a rainforest canopy, as rotund
as a pottery pitcher, as seamless

as a blown-glass jug, as porous
as cinnamon fern in a dawn drizzle.

If rows and rows of thin black
seeds lying in their canoe-shaped
pods atop multitudes of yuccas
scattered over the autumn plains
are countless, then every number
belongs to her.

And if bee plants and vase flowers,
ricebirds, whiptails, green
lacewings, frozen chorus toads, come
again and again, then she has always known
how to remain, promised, anointed,
her body, her face, the only one
in all our heavens, sole heiress
in whom we are very well pleased.

.   .   .   .   .

CONSIDER THE LILY

The obvious way first--blackberry, blue bead,
Easter and yellow pond, spider, swamp,
trout, rosetwisted, Indian cucumber,
colicroot.

Yet consider the lily a voice, its speech
carried blue-tipped, plaited and parallel
veined, rosette and basal murmur, alluring,
a seduction along peaty bog edges, moist
wooded slopes, meadows, through thickets,
over low sandy sites.

And look at lily––one "l" reaching
that way to the east, one "l" stretching
this way to the west––an embrace
it can never abandon.

Remember the lily moon, a full
flower every month; and the frothing
lily, there, never there, at the creek's
spill; and sugar lily/lily ice, spooned
and blooming in a silver bowl.

Consider *lily* on the tongue, a lullaby.
Lily. . . lily. . . it takes the sun, clucks
the light, makes a folded leaf
of fire.

Imagine the lily itself a tongue,
having become the white word it utters. *Lily*,
in fact, made flesh.

Picture the tongue a lily
saying *lily*. Such a smooth,
fragrant petal-licking it makes. One wants
to kiss it, bite it, suck it
to silence.

Say lily to me now then, luscious
flower. Don't you want to? Consider
a pure lily seduction––sarsaparilla,
featherbell, flesh and devil's bit,
zephyr, sessile. It could be perfect,
your basal tongue-lulling, lily-licking,
the moist thickets, the fold,
the froth, the rooted blooming
finally encompassed and in that moment
fully believed to be fully found.
Say *lily* to me now.

BECAUSE YOU UNDERSTAND THIS

Everything is watching you—the mockingbird,
the wood warbler, the jay, the crawfish frog,
carrion beetle, fungus beetle, the hanging fly;
everything is watching you, even the thick draw
of the tulip, the sunless center of the lidded
harebell bud, the underwater witch's nest—crowfoot,
bogbean—lungless salamander, the smallest circle
in the wound shell of the copper snail. Everything
stares. Each ring of the jingle shell, the stalk
of milk thistle, the blowing pine-needle
shadows reaching forward, forward and back,
on the stone walk, all are watching you.

Deep in its cave-stream, beneath its clear scale
and socket-skin, in its most impenetrable
unawareness, the eyeless glass fish attends,
and the tailless tenrec and the leaf-nosed
bat and the ruby mandrake in the dark
on the other side of the earth, even they,
and that which possesses only jawbone, naked
teeth in the north pasture, chipped femur
scattered vertebrae, that which possesses less
in the commodious muck of the pondbottom,
they too keep you in focus.

Everything, even the blind retina of underground
granite, even the ocular roll
of the thunderhead, even the solid
cold lens of the gray moon . . .

SUMMER SOLSTICE

When I was very, very fat, rotund
with hot hills and valleys, deep with purple
crevices and vapors, my belly a sizzling
horizon over which I could never see,
I sat on the old front porch on a patched
cushion, my puffed hands folded
across my steaming breasts.

I was bronze as a sun in those days, shining
with perspiration which often ran
like rain down the gully of my back, fell
occasionally toward evening in drops
like stars from my forehead.

Winter then was just a lacework
of bones, hardly a consideration
of skeleton buried deep and hidden
inside my bubbling and swirling,
my sweltering seethe.

I lay back, sank into my own blaze
and dozed, humming and snoring,
stirring a toe now and then, a twitch
of nose, all my keys turning, all my tressy
locks unlocked.

A citizenry of bumbles, a fiesta
of dragonflies in match-blue, in struck-gold,
whirled and hovered, pricked and darted
constantly about my girth. What a commotion
of blackbirds and flower pods rose
when I rumbled at noon, shifting slowly
from one gargantuan hip to the other.

I was so finely gorged, so beautifully
satiated. I sighed, pleased, rocked
and fantasized in the sheer breadth
of my own breathing, while one cool
green bead of bayou tree toad perched
crooning, lullabying low on the lip
and delve of my sheltering ear.

. . . . .

LANGUAGE AND EXPERIENCE

I consistently confuse the marsh frog
with the purple pitcher plant.
Maybe it's because each alike makes
a smooth spine of the light, a rounded
knot of forbearance from mud.

And which is blackbird? which prairie thistle?
They both latch on, glean, mind their futures
with numerous sharp nails and beaks.

Falling rain and water fleas are obviously
synonyms, both meaning *countless*
curling pocks of pond motion.
And aren't seeding cottonwood laces
and orb weavers clearly the same—clever
opportunists with silk?

I call field stars and field crickets
one and the other, because they're both
scattered in thousands of notches
throughout the night. And today I mistook
a blue creekside of lupine for *generosity,*
the way it held nothing back. O reed

canary grasses and *grace*—someone tell me
the difference again.

Write this down: my voice and a leaf
of aspen winding in the wind—we find the sun
from many spinning sides.

.   .   .   .   .

FIVE DIVINITIES OF RAIN
DURING SLEEP ALL NIGHT

I.

Turning once during sleep, I was certain
the rain was present. I might have perceived
a glinting measure of it then, like glimpsing
a gray slant of wing, an arc lost immediately
in all the other flying lines of the forest,
never comprehending the weights and graces
of the entire creature itself.

II.

And once after midnight, asleep,
I know I assumed the resonance
of rain particled among the poplar
leaves. I took in that quiet percussion
under my quilt, under my gown,
into my breastbone, into the smallest,
bone-sliver of audibility I possessed.
It rang there, many sided, hanging
with the same faltering cadence
found at the edges of star clusters
where neither rain nor tree nor
breastbone are ever found.

III.

I turned over. This is the way the rain
is sometimes during sleep: a shroud
the body knows is descending, shredded
and surfeiting and slow, so slow
in settling, never quite arriving
to cover and stop completely the mouth
and nose and eyes with a pressure
the body comes to wish for, a smothering
motion that sleep, even without a will,
longs to imitate.

IV.

All night I became the rain, multiple,
rolling over and over easily
off the roof edge, burning silver
and crooked on the glass outside,
wavering down through thunder, through
a theory of sky, down from the black
clouds, having possessed, before falling,
the moon in it shearing clarity high
above the other side of the same clouds.

V.

I almost remember having the rain
in my arms in bed last night, knowing
its real name finally, calling its real name
with its own tongue, pulling it down
and down, saying *god* once, sinking
with it piece by piece into the earth,
just the way we both always wanted.

JANUS

This is the body we know:
the one prolific with seeds, seeds
with translucent wings veined like dragonfly
wings, peach pits and poppy peppers,
seeds cradled in pods, emboweled
in birds, sky-flocking seeds of threaded
down looking like dixa midges circling
midair, swimming seeds with tails
like whips, seeds with teeth, seeds
with caskets, migrating seeds of needled
burrs and thistles, seeds like bits of ash
burning through the evening like flecks
of stars, and the dust-size seed of death
born in every heart coming to light.

This is the body we know:
the one moon-sterile, barren white
and barren black, bouldered with the frozen
rocks of dry polar plains and dusty drifts
of bristled snow, with gray, ancient
forests of fallen stone trunks and fronds,
littered with smoldering metal, shattered
meteors and melting iron, fossilized
spines and splintered bones, eyes locked
open and sightless in chunks of amber,
impotent, broken penes of marble, cracked
eggs of solid granite, and the rock-
permanent light of the heart born
in every seed rising to death.

THE DREAM OF THE MARSH WREN (1999)

THE DREAM OF THE MARSH WREN: RECIPROCAL CREATION

The marsh wren, furtive and tail-tipped,
by the rapid brown blurs of his movements
makes sense of the complexities of sticks
and rushes. He makes slashes and complicated
lines of his own in mid-air above the marsh
by his flight and the rattles of his incessant
calling. He exists exactly as if he were a product
of the pond and the sky and the blades of light
among the reeds and grasses, as if he were
deliberately willed into being by the empty
spaces he eventually inhabits.

And at night, inside each three-second
shudder of his sporadic sleep, understand
how he creates the vision of the sun
blanched and barred by the diagonal juttings
of the weeds, and then the sun as heavy
cattail crossed and tangled and rooted
deep in the rocking of its own gold water,
and then the sun as suns in flat explosions
at the bases of the tule. Inside the blink
of his eyelids, understand how he composes

the tule dripping sun slowly in gold rain
off its black edges, and how he composes
gold circles widening on the blue surface
of the sun's pond, and the sharp black
slicing of his wing rising against the sun,
and that same black edge skimming the thin
corridor of gold between sky and pond.

Imagine the marsh wren making himself
inside his own dream. Imagine the wren,
created by the marsh, inside the marsh
of his own creation, unaware of his being
inside this dream of mine where I imagine
he dreams within the boundaries of his own
fixed black eye around which this particular
network of glistening weeds and knotted
grasses and slow-dripping gold mist
and seeded winds shifting in waves of sun
turns and tangles and turns itself completely
inside out again here composing me
in the stationary silence of its only existence.

. . . . .

NUDE STANDING ALONE IN THE FOREST: A STUDY OF PLACE

In this unattached nudity, the certainty
of her bare feet pressed against the earth—sand-like
soil under the inner arch, essential pine needle
beneath the heel, blessed curl of old leaf—must seem
suddenly crucial. Completely unverified flesh
from the toes up, only the bottoms of her feet
can guess exactly where they are.

Naked for no one, it's obvious that nothing here,
not the noise of the wood warblers or the quiet
of the branch-tip spider or the poised stiffness
of the herb on which it rests, even in the sunlight,
takes particular notice of a bare breast. The wind
doesn't linger, moves steadily to its own places
among the upper leaves of the poplars no matter
what it touches of her on its way. And even outlined
perfectly in white against the background
of yaupon hedges, the curve of her hip and thigh
fitting exactly into their spaces before the wild grape,
her shoulder, as it should, marking the crucial arc
between dogwood and evening, it's still evident
that her body, unacknowledged, doesn't belong.
Uncaressed flesh by itself has no place
but anywhere.

Within this uncertain location of her unfound state,
staring up without a mirror, she can imagine
that she is the sky, as easy and open and accessible,
that her abode, therefore, is heaven.
Or she can believe that she is as undemanding
as the egret disappearing without looking back
over the far shore of the lake, that her habitation,
therefore, is wing. Or she can close her eyes and dream
that she is the motion in the perfect bud of hyacinth
slowly opening its blossom between her legs, petal
by petal to its fullest spread, that the only region
of her desire, therefore, is fantasy.

Yet even without a map it wouldn't be hard
for someone to find her here like this.
It wouldn't be hard for someone to create
the center of her as she creates the focus
of the forest which encircles him. And from
beneath the carefully descending darkness

of someone else, I know she could rise slowly
above all places like a soft, uncovered moon passing
through the thickest branches of the evening
as if the trees had no existence at all. I know
she possesses the power to change every
location of the night, if someone could only
find her inside his own arms right now
and discover where it is that this is so.

. . . . .

A SELF-ANALYSIS OF DUST

We know something about dust here on earth.
It makes its visible home in shafts of sunlight.
It can scatter unpredictably and float
in particles without wings. It can't be caught by hand.
It can find the tiny throats of every beggarweed
along the road. It can become the detectable funnel
of the wind. Sometimes dust can be gold.

Some people say dust represents the end,
the paltry evidence of a final dissolution.
It is considered a symbol of desertion when it lies
in long, empty corridors, a proof of degenerate
vacancy when it covers rose damask settees.
Its essence, as a result, is occasionally linked
with cold ashes.

But some say dust is the beginning,
its slow accumulation and eventual density in space
resulting in the formation of great rolling nebulae,
in the emergence of expansive galactic clusters,
the collapse of heavy stars into themselves. Dust,
in the right circumstances, can make its own light.

Some say our bodies are composed of the dust
of old stars, our minds are made from the dust
of old stars born and disintegrated billions
of years ago. If the atoms of our brains have
already experienced that beginning and that end,
if they have already accomplished that generation
of light, have already circumnavigated those far
reaches of blackness separated and alone, then
what vision is it we must always have seen
without realizing yet that we do?

Some people even believe that a measure of dust
of any kind, when blown upon by the proper breath,
can become a living soul. I wonder what soul
might be created if the light from a billion bright stars
were to be carefully gathered and measured
and blown upon here by living dust.

A few people are certain by the light
of their own minds and souls that dust knows
no time, being the one pure synthesis
of the beginning and the end.

. . . . .

THE GIFT OF RECEPTION

There is great kindness in reception.
Arthur, stretched still and stomach-flat,
is grateful for the wild guinea hen
who finally comes out of the willow to take
from his hand. There is a compliment
in the acceptance of that offering.

Some people believe they actually become the gift
they present, the spirit being united with the jade
figurine or caught circling in the silver ring
in its velvet case. Self-identity can be disguised
and presented as a lacquered mahogany box, a lace
shawl. If an ivory pendant or a grouping of wild
pinks and asters can become the physical
representation of the soul, then Cain,
Cain had valid motive.

Don't you understand that if you lie still,
if you take what I discover of your body,
if you accept what my fingertips can present to you
of your own face, how I might become what I give,
and how, by this investment, I might be bound
to keep seeking you forever?

This morning I want to give back the steep and rocky
ledge of this cold oak forest. I want to give back
the dense haze deepening further into frost
and the tight dry leaves scratching in the higher
cold. I want to give back my identity caught
in the expanding dimension of quiet found
by the jay. And with my soul disguised
as the wide diffusion of the sun behind the clouds,
I want to give back the conviction that light
is the only source of itself. I want these gifts
to be taken. I want to be invested in the one
who accepts them.

Maybe the most benevolent angel we can know
is the one whose body lies receptive, composed
of all the gifts we want most to give.

FOR THE FUTURE
EVOLUTION OF THE
GOD OF THE ABYSS

You who endures the repetitious
whipcrack and futile speed everywhere
stizzling in hapless, faltering

orbits, god of the hollow
at the core of the blasphemy
of the before and the blasphemy

of the final, being of and within
that void where sight cannot follow
and echo never returns, who is best

beheld in the unimagined
cavities of nameless oblivions
and temples of emptiness, who is

the never in all rantings
of extinction spat and stuttered
about like pieces of burnt newspaper

gusted down a winter street, the god
who is wrapped and bound and formed
by the question never formed,

the flame after the candle
is placed upside down in the dish,
you who bears your own vacuity

and your own nonentity, who retains
the essence of loss like a comet
in cycle bears and becomes the dust

of its own disintegration—within
the vast null and lack composing
your missing, remember us

made in your image, and then be
our pity, and then be our hope.

FROM

SONG OF THE WORLD BECOMING (2001)

(NEW POEMS IN *SONG OF THE WORLD BECOMING:*
NEW AND COLLECTED POEMS, 1981–2001)

A VERY COMMON FIELD

What is it about this grassy field
that's so familiar to me? Something
within the beings, the form of the place?
It's not within the foxtail, not within
the brome, not within oat grass or red clover
or yellow vetch or the lot of them as one
motion in the wind. It's not the morning
or even of the morning, or of the invisible
crickets, one near, one away, still sounding
in the damp after dawn.

What is it so resonant and recognized here?
A sense like nostalgia, a sense like manner,
like a state felt but not remembered?
It isn't the center of the purple cornflower
or its rayed and fluted edges, not the slow
rise of the land or the few scattered trees
left in the fallow orchard, not the stone path,
not the grains and bristles of stems and seeds,
each oblivious in its own business,
but something impossible without these.

It's more than the increasing depth
of the day and the blue of its height,
more than the half-body of the lizard
turned upside down on the path, torn
and transfigured during the night, more
than the bells beginning their lesson
in the background.

It's not a voice, not a message,
but something like a lingering,
a reluctance to abandon, a biding
so constantly present that I can never
isolate it from the disorderly crows
passing over or from the sun moving
as wind down through the brief fires
of moisture on the blades of timothy
and sage, never separate it from the scent
of fields drying and warm, never
isolate it from my own awareness.
It is something that makes possible,
that occasions without causing, something
I can never extricate to name, never
name to know, never know to imitate.

. . . . .

BEING SPECIFIC

The beginning subject is narrowed
first to the yellow toe-claw on the left
front seven-segmented leg of this one
specific, totally bright yellow
spider misplaced, a small spectacle
moving across the damp, grey
gravel of the forest path.

Yet the subject, more specifically,
is the cellular tremble of pulse
in this particular toe-claw belonging
to this very spider I see, lost
from its yellow-orange flowerfield--
goldenrod, daisy, jessamine.

Still, to be more exact, the sole
subject here is one colorless shiver
of molecule inside the one-chambered
heart of this quite shiny, yellow-
eyed, golden pea-orb pausing
on rock at my feet.

But the focus, to designate
further, must be on one atom-
to-atom link inside this arachnid
heart this afternoon, and further,
within this spider-atom, one electron,
and beyond that, one hadron, one quark,
and further beyond that, the last
and finest specification possible,
which is naturally the only
underlying, indivisible universal
that thus possesses like the void
and exhibits like the boundless
and holds distance like the night
and serves like the sun and inhabits
like the stars and therefore exists
as this split-moment's revelation
inside the mind meeting itself
in the recognition of its own
most specific composition.

THE NATURE OF
THE HUCKSTER

Put on his garment of rain,
came swaying in silver across
the garden, his fragrance
of clarity preceding him. Put on
his garment of theft, stole
the seeds of the pecan, the eggs
of the horseshoe crab, roe
of cod, roe of mackerel, stole
the children's gold and purple
marbles, stole breath, stole fever.
Filled his pockets with blood.
Filled his pockets with charity.
Emptied his pockets of confetti-
feathers and bones. Emptied

his pockets of beetle menageries.
Over his garment of snow, donned
his garment of sun. Over his
many-colored coat of deception,
put on his many-colored robe
of verisimilitude. Under his attire
of aridity, wore his thunder cloak
of deluge. Put on his robe
of celibacy. Put on his jewelry
of prostitution. Traded his
garment of frivolity. Bartered
his overcoat of constancy. Shucked
his shawl of grief. Threw off
his hood of sanity. Under his silk

cape of surrender, clothed himself
in his steel vestment of siege.
Put on his garment of disdain. Covered
himself in his rags of spring. Wrapped
himself in his blankets of faith.
Discarded his garment of life. Donned
his garment of death. Put on his
garment of matter. Took off
his garment of light. Discarded
his garment of decay. Put on
his garment of lies. Paraded
back and forth, plain and invisible
in his ruse of apparel, hawking,
all the while, himself. Take him.

. . . . .

ON THE WAY TO EARLY
MORNING MASS

I entered the sea on the way
to early morning mass, walked
down deep along the rims of rock
coral caverns where my misstep
and consequent falling was most
slow and careful flying. I passed
over fields of slender, swaying
tubes of cuttlefish nests, supple
sheaves white and iridescent as pearl,
moved among the swift metal precision
of barracuda passion and shears.
A scatter of rain on the ceiling
of the sea above me appeared a sky-wide
scatter of stars struck to light
and snuffed in the same moment.

I rose from the sea on the way
to early morning mass, walked along
the wet stones of the path, through
the sunken-blue-eyed grasses and cat
peas of the pasture gauzed with drizzled
webs, shrouds and shells of beeflies
and seeds clinging to my feet,
along the two-rutted road, its frost-
fringed skims of water in shallow
delves, the fence ragged and tipsy
with wild rose, stripped blossoms,
crusty yellow leaves black-spotted.

On the way to early morning mass,
I entered the soft-spun skull inside
the curlew's egg, heard the echo
of chimes in that electric cellar
of sun, entered the knot of the witch's
pit, the sweet pulp pit of the lover's
intention, the knot of felicity,
the pit of vagary. Nothing was blacker
fire than the government of summer
collapsed in the knot of the coal.

I passed once a fragrance
of strawberries and orange simmering
for jam, once lavender and cedar
as from a spinster's trunk long
locked and suddenly opened, once
a sage wind down from the tops
of the pines. A door blew shut,
and a mongrel bitch on her chain
yipped to an empty window, circled
twice on her measured length.

On the way to early morning mass,
I followed the invisible corridor
of sky forged by swallows from river
bank to bluff, followed the way
of my hand along the bones of his sleep
in bed beside me, followed the way
of my eye following the way of winter
rain down the icy runnels of budded
oak, and every remembered motion
of succeeding motion was providential,
the way of making the way sanctum,
the proceeding the arrival,
the service continuing on
the continuing.

.   .   .   .   .

BELIEVING IN BLOOD

I don't know how fast the blood
must rush through the throat, up
the spinal column, round the gut
and lungs and ribs of the sparrow's
three-ounce body. I don't know how fast
it must speed, the color of fire unseen
below ground, maybe almost smoking,
that blood careening back from wing tip,
back from claw nail and brow, back
to the pow of the heart keeping
the body an ember in this Arctic blue
air that breaks and seizes with zero.

Maybe in harsh moments like these
the blood flies as fast inside a bird's
boundaries as a rock shot past a high

cliff plummets toward the sharp
water of the ice-rimmed rush below.
Maybe the blood winding inside a bird's
body in January cold moves as fast
and as forcefully as the arc of a whip
flicked high, sparking across a frozen
sky, melting the threatening strictures
of winter with the heat of its own racing.

The sparrow gleans and prims among the icy
weeds, hardly noticing, as if she knew
she were not merely herself, not pulse,
not marrow, not throbbing, but an eternal
equation of motion relative to belief
relative to loss that always results,
anywhere it figures in the heavens,
in a tight fist of feathers,
bone-red structures and breath.

The enduring, absolute math
of this sparrow must exist right now
elsewhere, replicated a billion other
times as wire feet, beak pricking,
shocking shaft of eye present
in the swirl of forces roaring
through the igniting star bombs
and radiances among which we float.

The intricate shadows of winter branches
networked across the snow plain
where I stand seem to me now the flat
black veins of missing birds who long ago
must have mistakenly abandoned forever
their faith in the calculation
of momentum and promise present
in a crimson of salt.

SPEAKING OF EVOLUTION:
LUMINOSITY

For aren't we all the children
of the children of great-grandfathers
who called down lightning, who sought out
the tree struck and smoldering, who minded
the punk log day and night as if it
were alive? We are each of us the progeny
of grandmothers who guarded burning
rocks held in seashells, who cradled
coals in clay cups through windy mountain
journeys; the sons and daughters
of mothers who blew sparks on twisted
moss wicks floating in bowls of oil;
the family of those who peeled
bark strips from trailside trees,
twined and lit the funnels to burn
as torches on rainy night treks.
We are kin to the kin of fathers
who spun wood against wood until
the smoky heat ignited fine-thread
tinder of cedar hairs, charred
corn tassels, who fanned and coddled
and spoke to the warm light coming.

The old structures of these ritual
passions, kept deep in the genes,
in the heart—like precious scripts
preserved in the rock cellars of hidden
monasteries—these are eternal. They breathe,
alive in the seed of every coming child,
each tiny embryo skeleton bound
and forming to fit forever the bones
and powers of all past solicitors of light.

And during any cold, frightful time
when something of vision is missing,
these talents will appear, rising,
seeming of a sudden resurrected--
the way inert soil opened to sun seems
of a sudden to flower--the kindling,
the watchful nursing, the urging forth
of that first slight savior of flame,
the same close kissing of fire,
as if, in truth, the earth had never
been absolved without such religion.

.   .   .   .   .

BORN OF A RIB
Genesis 2:21, 22

Maybe it was actually from the delicate
rib of a piñon mouse put to a deep
sleep just for this purpose in his bed
of shredded juniper bark, or from
the steadfast bone of a snoring boar,
that chest stave as tough and stone-
mandatory as one of his searing tusks.

Sometimes it seems the making
must have originated in the edifying
rib of a fern leaflet drowsy
before dawn, because the satiating
taste of its earth-subtle sap
still lingers in the mouth. Yet
there is evidence that the forming
came from the marrow blood of a blue
whale's rib, because the regular
thunder of his near heart remains

permanent and dictatorial in the sound
of time passing in its orbits.

There are moments when I could imagine
emerging, gyring and firmament-rounded,
made soaring by the hollow bone
of a broad-winged hawk in his element,
or being turned upside down, born
subterranean, sun-denying and recalcitrant
from the dormant rib of a brown bat
in his cave hibernation.

Everything might be different today,
we could agree, if the rib chosen
had been taken from the shell
of the somnolent rosy cockle,
so steadfastly sculpted, so smoothly
sea-polished, so stoically pure,
or if the insistent, violet rib
of the rainbow had been the one selected,
or if the false transparent rib
of the night's vaulted sleep had been
the one extracted for the purpose.

But in truth—remember—from whatever
spine of creature, plant, or sky-cage
the said material rib was stolen,
to that alone must belong forever
all the blessing, all the blame.

VENERATION

What is it in the body that wants
to go on living, that heals the wound,
that knits the bone even while the I
is sleeping, that takes air to blood
unnoticed while the singer prays
for grace, while the thief darts in
and out pedestalled doorways,
while the player plucks the guitar,
while the reader deserts his own
to enter the book?

Not summoned, what is it in the body
that quickens by itself, goes sharp
and dimensional at near thunder, that lifts
and lightens in the presence of laughter
across a lawn, purple and rose lanterns
strung through trees at dusk?

Is it just an emptiness, like the motion
of an empty cape that undulates
and flutters at its edges as it flies,
like the emptiness inside the cape
of the midnight wind, inside the fluttering
shadow-cape of the manta ray flying
across the ocean floor? Maybe it's just
a nothingness like the vision of lightning
to the blind--never known, only remembered.

But it stays a place. It genders
warmth. It contrives. It is as tangible
and exact as the *stone* of a stone idol,
as straight and alert as a ghost riding
a riderless stallion. It creates like sunlight

on water makes fire. It maintains
as if its message were entire in simply
making message possible.

What is it in the body that wants
to stay alive, that itself has no name
except *keeper,* except *vigilance,* except
above all, except *undeniable?*

. . . . .

AFTERWARD

I caress the bony, bald forehead
of his skull, soothing, riveling
along its cracked boundaries,
and trace his eye pits, round
and round each rim, penetrating
the nether black of those two
bottomless bolt holes.

I gather together and spread
his fleshless finger-sticks, open
and shut them like the staves
of a fan. They click together
with a sound like ivory dice shaken
in a wooden cup. Occasionally I push
the teeth apart, widen the jaw
and look in and out the other
side, the mossy white vertebrae
of his craggy neck.

Once the moon was in his mouth
like an apple in the mouth
of a roasted pig. Once a moment

of moth settled in the space
for his tongue. Once the shadows
and suns of cedars and fronds
were ancestries shining from the spaces
of his head. Was it the scholastic
current of the stars I then thought
he held in his hands?

I lick up and down and up
his spine, cuddle him, cradle him
on my lap, his bare pelvis bowl
slipping. I turn his clatter over
and turn it back. I bend his knee
joints, let his foot bones dangle
like fish on a line. I grip the grate
of his empty ribs and raise the whole
contraption of his being clacking
and rattling in its own confusion.
Down it tangles, bobbing and guttering.
Remember, it is I alone who enter
through the staves of his hollow
framework, rub and beat steadily
where his heart once rumbled.

His reason is the only form
of my madness; for, heaven ever above,
he is measure and I am flow, he is
earth and I am sea.

THE BLESSINGS OF
ASHES AND DUST

Cuckoo birds and putterings of wrens
bathe in them, showering themselves
luxuriantly, making small riots
in dry ditches or old, black campfires.
Web-footed geckos and sidewinders are glad
to bury in their powders, and the back-flip
spider weaves them into her web
then pulls it over her body
to hide on the desert from her prey.

Not at all like water, air, icy smoke
or fog, they both, while still basic
and elemental, can yet be held easily
in the hands. And most pleasantly
obscure, unlike fossils of mammoths
or jawless fishes, dust and ashes
hardly resemble in the least
what they used to be.

So totally dead, there's no fear
of more death in either. They thus possess
a sublimity far beyond the frenetic
wolverine, the nervous, ever-vigilant,
meerkats, and they can maintain a lasting
serenity never hoped for by a bloom
of yellow meadow rue or a powdery
blue wing of prairie ringlet.

And ashes and dust are esteemed,
being cited in scripture (ashes
over the body for anguish, dust shaken
off the heels for scorn). They are called on

by name often in grief, sometimes even kept
in honored marble jars in locked and honored
places. They have been wept over
by most everyone from the beginning.

Surely dependable, these two never change
their natures suddenly to something else
radically different, as a pignut
hickory seed is known to do, and likewise
a white, breast-warmed phoebe egg
in its mossy nest.

In a world of shift, fall, mirage,
hallucination, swindle, and evil
trickery, this certainty must be
considered a blessing: pure ashes
and dust alone forever remain
thoroughly themselves, so ever
and ever and ever.

.   .   .   .   .

STONE BIRD

I remember you. You're the one
who lifted your ancient bones
of fossil rock, pulled yourself free
of the strata like a plaster figure
rising from its own mold, became
flesh and feather, took wing,
arrested the sky.

You're the one who, though marble,
floated as beautifully as a white
blossom on the pond all summer,

who, though skeletal and particled
like winter, glimmered as solid as a bird
of cut crystal in the icy trees.

You are redbird—sandstone
wings and agate eyes—at dusk.
You are greybird—polished granite
and pearl eyes—just before dawn,
midnight bird with a reflective
vacancy of heart like a mirror
of pure obsidian.

You're the one who flew down
to that river from the heavens,
as if your form alone were the only
holy message needed. You were alabaster
then in the noonday sun.

Once I saw you rise without rising
from your prison pedestal
in the garden beneath the lime tree.
At that moment your ghost
in its haunting permeated every
regality of the forest with light,
reigned with disdain in thin air
above the mountain, sank in union
with the crosswinds of the sea.

I remember you. You're the one
who entered in through my death
as if it were an open window
and you were the sound of the serenade
being sung outside for me, the words
of which, I know now, are of freedom
cast in stone forever.

MILLENNIUM MAP OF THE
UNIVERSE (FROM THE
*NATIONAL GEOGRAPHIC
SOCIETY)*

It's a beautiful heaven, shining aqua
arrangements on black, scattered
chips of pure turquoise, gold, sterling
white, ruby sand, dimmer clouds
of glowing stellar dust, beads
like snow, like irregular pearls.

Last week, I thought this heaven was
god's body burning, as in the burning
bush never consumed, sudden flarings
of the omnipresence, the coal tips
of god's open hand, the brilliance of god's
streaming hair, the essence of grace
in flames, the idea of creation illuminated.
I believed each form of light and darkness
in that combustion was the glorious
art of god's body on fire, the only
possible origin of such art. Maybe god's
body remains invisible until it ignites
into its beginning. I could almost detect
the incense rising from such transfiguration.

But yesterday I believed it was music,
the circling and spiraling of sound
in a pattern of light, a design I might
begin to perceive, each note, each count
and measure of the concert-in-progress
being visible, constellations of chords,
geysers of scales, the bell-like lyricism
of overlapping revolutions and orbits, deep

silent pauses of vacancy, as we might
expect, among the swells and trills,
the cacophony of timpani, the zinking
of tight strings. Yesterday this seemed
a reasonable thought, a pleasing
thought. It seemed possible.

Today, I see it is just signal numbers,
static and spate: the sun, 25,000 light-
years from the center of "our galactic
realm" around which we travel once
every 200 million years, you understand.
I don't resist the calculated mass of "our
supercluster." I don't deny those 100
trillion suns of our suns among which
we pass, turning over and over day
after night after day. The last "outpost"
in our cluster, before a desert cosmic
void begins, is named Virgo. I stop there
for rest and provisions, to water the horses,
pour oats in their trough, to cradle my child.

I wish I could sing like electrons
on a wheel. I wish I could burn
like god.

. . . . .

THE STARS BENEATH MY FEET

Not the burrowing star-nosed
mole or the earth roots of the star-
thistle or the yellow star flowers
of star grass, not the fallen webs
and empty egg sacs of star-bellied

spiders, not blood stars or winged
sea stars tight on their tidal rock
bottoms, and I don't mean either
the lighted star-tips of the lantern
fish and angler fish drifting
miles deep at the ocean's end
of their forever good night.

I mean those actual stars filling
the skies directly below me with ignited
hubs and knotted assemblies combusting
into the waves of their own momentum,
the same stars in kind as the ones
above—gaseous blue clusters of clouds
expelling hot super stellars, fusing
galaxy upon galaxy of old histories
and reverberations. Those stars.

Were the earth made of glass,
any of us could look down now and see
them speeding away deeper into their vast
eras of math and glory existing immediately
beneath us where we stand suspended.

Even while marsh rains slowly
fill the hoofprints of passing
deer, even while flocks of lark
and longspur fly across the evening
with accordion motions of fracture
and union, even while you, fragranced
with sleep, draw me close or send me out,
stars and myriads of stars possess
their places, surrounding us as if
their facts bore us upward from below,
sheltered us in matrices of invisible
canopies above, as if they graced us

with a balance manifest in their far
numbers extending away equally
on our left and on our right.
They are the designated ancestors
of our eyes created in the lasting
moments of their own dead light.
They keep us on all sides bound safe
within their spheres and apart
from that great dire and naught
existing beyond the measurable
edges of their established dominions.

.   .   .   .   .

SELF-RECOGNITION OF THE OBSERVER AS MOMENTARY CESSATION OF PROCESS

1.

Surrounded by great thunder-floods
and rending storms, a small face,
wrinkled as a peach pit, is seen
for an instant in the sky, wild hair
and bountiful beard the whipping
manes of rainclouds and winds.
A split-second reflection of stillness
and pause, it disappears at once
into the wide tangle of the fracas
covering the heavens.

2.

Within the family portrait, a circle
of painted mirror above the mantle
reveals the artist at work both within

and beyond the frame and reveals
as well the window behind the artist,
outside which paned glass a moon
cat with round yellow mirrors
for eyes sits looking back through
the moment when we first perceive
the center and the score
of the before and the after.

3.

From a train traveling
through a midnight countryside,
one might glimpse on a distant
hill a hut, scarcely detectable
in its passing speed. Inside,
a tailor, by lantern-light
at his machine, bends over a single
stitch, then vanishes into the unseen
needle and wheel of the proceeding
history of his work.

4.

A cliff swallow soaring above the river
stops mid-sky, not hovering, but ceasing
all movement—negative-beat, negative-
breath—a bird-conjunction of the recognized
everywhere, before descending again
into the rage and vacuum of the rock
canyon below.

ONCE UPON A TIME, WHEN I WAS ALMOST DEAD WITH FEAR AND DOUBT

I cavorted with my harp. I recovered her
first from the closet, dusted and polished
the curves and flowers of her finely
molded architecture, tuned and tightened
her most subtle nuances. I twirled her
gracefully round and round on her one toe,
bending her toward the ground until
we almost kissed and then raising her again
in a swirl, as if from the dead, plucking
her many little tones all the while.

Me in my patent leather slippers,
she in fake furs and feathers wrapped
about her slender neck, I danced her
out across the flat grey surface
of the sea, farther and farther, never
looking down, as one is advised,
keeping my eyes steadily on the narrow
rim of distant earth beyond. I nearly
swooned, strumming and strumming
her many little teases and woebegones
in time to the waves. Such whispers,
such rocking hushes and sighs.

Landing on the opposite shore,
we had our picture made, she nestling
on my breast, me aglow, my arms
around her golden body. She hummed,
off and on, little snatches of senseless
tunes, engaging various keys and octaves
with the winds on the cliffs above that sea-

side village. Together all the moonless night,
I held her up to the heavens. I brought
her close. I sang to her, plinking
the many little silver scales and stars
I saw shining between the strings
of her soul. She was a-shimmer,
a perfect trembling array. I listened.

And with the morning, in short,
I returned recovered, stashed her away
again in the same closet where I keep
the painted, wooden horse on wheels,
the paper kite with yellow wings,
my mask of the moon, the top that spins
and wobbles and falls and spins.

.   .   .   .   .

ALMANAC

When Jesus the Christ was born,
it was the anniversary of the day
the last living dinosaur crumpled,
fell to the ground like a giant
sequoia, died in its bones,
and ceased.

On the day Jesus the Messiah
was born, the grand river-sea,
Rio Amazonas, nearly white, as usual,
with light-reflecting particles
of suspended clay, flowed along
steadily toward its confluence
with the Rio Negro.

The crater rocks lay
just as we see them tonight
on the moonlight side of the moon,
when the King of Kings first
came to be. But the Leonid shower
of two hundred thousand meteors
was traveling still centuries
from earth, and Krakatau loomed
serene, benign, without murder,
in the southern sea.

At the same hour the infant Jesus
of Nazareth first drew breath,
Great China went forth in imperial
parade and regalia, a wagon of bronze
chimes rolling and ringing like sun
on a river in full morning, and a lone
zither, played in the countryside,
was tapped by the left finger
of the solitary musician, and so sounded
"the echo of an empty valley."

On the night of the day the Savior
was born, a mother Marie, her first infant
daughter stillborn, died alone in childbirth
in a dark stable on the other side
of another realm of another plane.

On the day of the first Christmas,
sea elephant cows lolled in fat harems
among snorting bulls guarding
their western sandy beaches, and cannibals
blessed and ate in the land of tinkerbirds,
pottos, bush pigs, and drongos, and a caracal
on the desert carefully licked clean

the crevices of each of her bloody claws,
and unnamed winds ravaged the rock-
ice pinnacles of the Himalayas,

and the presentiment of illusory union
moves closer and moves farther away
and passes through from the center onward.

. . . . .

WATCHING THE ANCESTRAL
PRAYERS OF VENERABLE
OTHERS

Lena Higgins, 92, breastless,
blind, chewing her gums by the window,
is old, but the Great Comet of 1843

is much older than that. Dry land
tortoises with their elephantine
feet are often very old, but giant

sequoias of the western Sierras
are generations older than that.
The first prayer rattle, made

on the savannah of seeds and bones
strung together, is old, but the first
winged cockroach to appear on earth

is hundreds of millions of years
older than that. A flowering plant
fossil or a mollusk fossil in limy

shale is old. Stony meteorites buried
beneath polar ice are older than that,
and death itself is very, very

ancient, but life is certainly older
than death. Shadows and silhouettes
created by primordial sea storms

erupting in crests high above
one another occurred eons ago,
but the sun and its flaring eruptions

existed long before they did. Light
from the most distant known quasar
seen at this moment tonight is old

(should light be said to exist
in time), but the moment witnessed
just previous is older than that.

The compact, pea-drop power
of the initial, beginning nothing
is surely oldest, but then the intention,

with its integrity, must have come
before and thus is obivously
older than that. Amen.

BEFORE THE BEGINNING:
MAYBE GOD AND A SILK
FLOWER CONCUBINE PERHAPS

The white sky is exactly the same white
stone as the white marble of the transparent
earth, and the moon with its clear white
swallow makes of its belly of rock neither
absence nor presence.

The stars are not syllables yet enunciated
by his potential white tongue, its vestigial
lick a line that might break eventually,
a horizon curving enough to pronounce
at last, my love.

The locked and frigid porcelain barrens
and hollows of the descending black plain
are a pattern of gardens only to any single
blind eye blinking, just as a possible stroke
of worm, deaf with whiteness, might hear
a lace bud of silk meridians spinning
and unraveling simultaneously on the vacuous
beds of the placeless firmament.

An atheist might believe in the seductive
motion turning beneath the transparent gown
covering invisibly the non-existent bones
and petals of no other. Thus the holy blossom,
spread like the snow impression of a missing
angel, doubts the deep-looped vacancy
of her own being into which god, in creation,
must assuredly come.

Is it possible there might be silver seeds
placed deep between those legs opening
like a parting of fog to reveal the plunging salt
of a frothy sea? But god digresses, dreaming
himself a ghost, with neither clamor nor ecstasy,
into inertia, his name being farther
than ever from time.

Static on the unendurably boring white
sheet of his own plane, he must think hard
toward that focus of conception when he can rise
shuddering, descending and erupting into the beauty
and fragrance of their own making together--
those flowering orange-scarlet layers and sun-
shocking blue heavens of, suddenly, one another.

.   .   .   .   .

THE BACKGROUND BEYOND
THE BACKGROUND

On an autumn afternoon, perhaps selecting
apples from a crate or examining pickled beets
and onions in a jar, or watching two honeybees
at one red clover, we stand unaware
before a background of behest and sanctity.

Or floating down a river through elm
and cottonwood shadows, past sandbar
willows and lines of turtles on sunning logs,
over underwater thickets, bottom beds
of leaf roughage and mud, we are, all the while,
made finely distinct upon a more distant
background of singularity.

Anywhere we turn, this background
stays, a domain for mortal and immortal,
for crystal grids, for shifting furls of smoke,
for structure and fallibility, for each nexus
of sword and cross.

Atop a barn roof, a glossy green-tailed
rooster with auburn feathers lifts his wings
against a backdrop of dawn. Is it the passing
moment of occupied event or the passing fact
of barnyard morning that creates the impression
of presence before this silk of elusive
light behind light?

Like a clear horizon at the edge of a wide
field, the background beyond the background
of sky reveals most explicitly the figures
of those that come before it--elephant
or ostrich or seed-heavy grasses, saint,
sow, runt or sire, summer lightning,
blowing ice. It achieves us all.

Far, far beyond those far mountains of stone
and cavern against which I am outlined now
there is another background--translucent,
stolid, eloquent, still.

FROM

GENERATIONS (2004)

GENERATIONS

They have been walking from the beginning,
through the foggy sponges of lowland
forests, under umbrella leaves, in the shattered
rain of ocean beaches, through the tinder
of ash pits, the thickets of cities, along washes
and ravines and the dust of dry creek beds.

When the great ice mountain split
its continent and became two, they were walking.
When smoke from the burning plains
blinded the western seas, they were walking.
They walked by dead reckoning on steel,
on ropes, over swales and fens, on pearls.

They passed through congregations
of meteors, through knots of flies,
and howling tangles of hungry winds.
When they were sleeping on moss,
they were walking. When they lay
broken, torn and still on the field,
they were walking. They were walking
when the sun gathered together the tightening
strings of its slack, when the sun dissolved
into the withering circle of its power.

An old dog trailed them off and on,
and flocks of ricebirds and their shadows
rose up and scattered before them. Herds
of holy caribou and hosts of preying
wolves disappeared ahead of them
over the snowy hills. They were walking
with ghosts, with choirs of grasses
and armies of stars. They walked
through the words *let there be light*
more than once. They were walking
with chronicles of chains. They walked beyond
the headwaters of the moon.

And people saw them coming and people
saw them passing, and their walking
was constant, unmoving, invariable,
and the seeing of the people was ever
present, immutable, liberation.

.   .   .   .   .

A TRAVERSING

The easy parting of oaks and hickories,
bays of willows, borders of pine and screens
of bamboo down to the crux, grasses, bulrushes
and reeds parting down to their fundamental
cores, the yielding of murky pond waters,
layer upon layer giving way to the touch

of the right touch, the glassy, clear
spring waters, bone and gristle alike
opening as if opening were ultimate fact,
the parting of reflection allowing passage,
and the cold, amenable skeleton of echo,
the unlatching of *marsh* becoming as easily

accessible as the unlocking of *mercy*,
as the revelation of stone splitting
perfectly with the sound of the right
sound, everything, a nubbin of corn,
a particle of power, the pose of the sky
relenting, and the sea swinging open

like the doors of a theater giving entrance
to everyone, no fences, no barriers, no blinds
to the parting of the abyss, not bolted,
not barred from the utmost offering
of the dusk, enigma itself falling away
until all may enter all and pass among them.

. . . . .

ALPHA AND OMEGA

Three blackbirds tear at carrion
in a ditch, and all the light
of the stars is there too, present
in their calls, embodied in their ebony
beaks, taken into the cold wells
of their eyes, steady on the torn
strings of rotten meat in the weeds.

Starlight pierces the sea
currents and crests, touching scuds
and krill and noble sand amphipods.
It moves so steadily it is stationary
through the swill of seaweed, the fleshy
shells of purple jellyfish.

And all the light from star masses,
from constellations and clusters,

surrounds the old man walking
with his stick at night tapping the damp.
The light from those sources
exists in his beginning, interwoven
with his earliest recollections--
phrase of cradle and breath, event
of balance and reach.

Light from the stars is always
here, even with the daytime sun,
among cattle on coastal plains
and the egrets riding on their backs,
shining on the sky-side of clouds
and straight through the fog of clouds,
between white fox and white hare,
between each crystal latch to crystal
in snow. It illuminates turreted
spires and onion domes of foreign
cities, enters the stone mouths
and grimaces of saints and gargoyles,
touches the mossy roofs of weathered
barns, insect-tunneled eaves and the barbs
of owls, and all sides of each trunk
and shadow-blossom of bee trees
and willow banks, filling orchards
and aisles of almonds and plums.

The starlight comes, in union
and multiple, as weightless
as the anticipation of the barest
rain, as the slightest suggestion
of a familiar voice sounding
in the distance. It is as common,
as fulsome as the air of a mellow
time with no wind. The light
of the stars encompasses everything,

even until and beyond the final cold
passing of the last cinder-bone
and minim of the vanished earth.

. . . . .

THE PASSING OF THE
WISE MEN

They collected them one by one
like seed-size pearls and put them
in their black velvet bags, gathered
them like small marbles of amethyst
and alabaster, plucked them
like white cherries from a tree.

They placed all of them carefully
in their velvet bags scarcely filled.
And they were patient, gathering
them slowly all their lives, some
like berries of glass, like the slighter
fruit of mistletoe, some appearing
like tiny flames flashing on sunless
river bottoms or shining like quick silver
schools of fish in the deep. A few
were as cold and black and enigmatic
as skull sockets where eyes should be.

When the end came, they crawled
into their black velvet sacks themselves,
pulled the drawstrings tight over
their heads, looked around and above
in the speckled dark and more than once
toward the east, then assembled
their instruments and resumed the study

of their everlasting treasures ⸺Sirius,
Polaris, Arcturus, Capella, Vega,
Andromeda, Cygnus X, guides,
messengers, hope.

.   .   .   .   .

SERVANT, BIRTHRIGHT

If god was a cow, I could lead him
by a rope through a ring in his nose,
hang a bell around his neck, always
hear him wherever he was, even alone
in the open night. I could feed him
and fatten him. I could take him to clover
and fields of new grasses, put hay
on the snow for him in winter. I could
walk him to shelter out of hailstones
and thunderstorms, through the smoke
of summer fires, past trailing wolves, free him
from thorny bramble and cactus patches.

If god was a cow, I could slaughter him.
I could bludgeon him in the head
between the eyes with a hammer,
crack his skull, see his brains seeping.
I could watch his legs crumple under him
as he sank to the ground. I could feel
in the shake of the earth, and remember,
the weight of him as he fell.

I could eat him, drain his blood,
cook his blood and spoon it in
like soup. I could roast him, savor
his flanks and ribs and simmering

fat, absorb his fragrances, the perfumes
of his waft and smoke. I could skin him
and tan his hide and fashion his hide
and wear his hide as shoes, as hat,
as weskit, be covered by the pelt
of god, walk inside of god.

I could say, "I know you, god.
It was I who named you *cow*.
I have kept you, prepared you,
honored you, watched over you.
I have borne witness to you. After all,
I butchered you with care and skill.
I cut you open to the core. I uncovered
your parts. I touched all of your parts,
your secret parts. I have tasted you,
chewed you up, swallowed you,
sucked your bones and spit them out,
bleached your empty skull and hung it
high on my wall. I have wanted
you. I have needed you. You
have become and forsaken me.
In this we must both be satisfied."

.   .   .   .   .

THE BODY AND THE SOUL

Coming, cursing, with his stick raised,
he routs the geese from the garden,
the chickens from the kitchen, the phantom
from the marsh, the alleyway. Swinging
and swishing, he thrashes severely
the fearsome nothing behind the door.

He uses the stick in April to draw
furrows, to prod, to make spaces
in the plowed earth where he plants
pieces of potato, seeds of carrots,
corn, marigold.

In the forest, he flips over a stone
with his stick, beneath which we find
eleven pill bugs, one white spider, a hard,
glistening spot of land snail. With the tip
of the stick, he discovers and touches
lightly the fleshy stem of the wild celery,
the pungent rootstock of the sweet flag.

He measures the depth of the pool,
lowering the stick straight down
to the bottom where the mud
salamander settles and the brown clam
lies. Almost submerged entirely,
it's nearly lost in the process.

He holds it to his eye in the field.
He sights along its length to find true
north, to fix our location. With his stick
he can strike the cross of the coordinates
exactly. He can write directions
in soft soil or sands.

At night he holds it high as it points
to Rigel, Capella, the Great Galaxy
in Andromeda. He circles it above
his head to trace the diurnal motion
of the stars around Polaris.

Later, he hobbles a little. He leans
on his stick. It makes his way home.

IN GENERAL

This is about no rain in particular,
just any rain, rain sounding on the roof,
any roof, slate or wood, tin or clay
or thatch, any rain among any trees,
rain in soft, soundless accumulation,
gathering rather than falling on the fir
of juniper and cedar, on a lace-community
of cobwebs, rain clicking off the rigid
leaves of oaks or magnolias, any kind
of rain, cold and smelling of ice or rising
again as steam off hot pavements
or stilling dust on country roads in August.
This is about rain as rain possessing
only the attributes of any rain in general.

And this is about night, any night
coming in its same immeasurably gradual
way, fulfilling expectations in its old
manner, creating heavens for lovers
and thieves, taking into itself the scarlet
of the scarlet sumac, the blue of the blue
vervain, no specific night, not a night
of birth or death, not the night forever
beyond the frightening side of the moon,
not the night always meeting itself
at the bottom of the sea, any sea, warm
and tropical or starless and stormy, night
meeting night beneath Arctic ice.
This attends to all nights but no night.

And this is about wind by itself,
not winter wind in particular lifting
the lightest snow off the mountaintop

into the thinnest air, not wind through
city streets, pushing people sideways,
rolling ash cans banging down the block,
not a prairie wind holding hawks suspended
mid-sky, not wind as straining sails
or as curtains on a spring evening, casually
in and back over the bed, not wind
as brother or wind as bully, not a lowing
wind, not a high howling wind. This is
about wind solely as pure wind in itself,
without moment, without witness.

Therefore this night tonight—
a midnight of late autumn winds shaking
the poplars and aspens by the fence, slamming
doors, rattling the porch swing, whipping
thundering black rains in gusts across
the hillsides, in batteries against the windows
as we lie together listening in the dark, our own
particular fingers touching—can never
be a subject of this specific conversation.

.   .   .   .   .

A STATEMENT OF CERTAINTY

Here we are, all of us now, some of us
in emerald feathers, in chestnut or purple,
some with bodies of silver, red,
or azure scales, some with faces
of golden fur, some with sea-floating
sails of translucent blue, some pulsing
with fluorescence at dusk, some
pulsing inside shell coverings shining
like obsidian, or inside whorled

and spotted spindle shells, or inside
leaves and petals folded and sealed
like tender shells.

Because many of us have many names—
black-masked or black-footed or blue-
footed, spiny, barbed, whiskered or ringed,
three-toed, nine-banded, four-horned,
whistling or piping, scavenger or prey—
we understand this attribute of god.
Because some of us, not yet found, possess
no names of any kind, we understand,
as well, this attribute of god.

All of us are here, whether wingless
clawless, eyeless, or legless, voiceless,
or motionless, whether hanging
as pods of fur and breath in branches
knitted over the earth or hanging
from stone ceilings in mazes of hallways
beneath the earth, whether blown across
oceans trailing tethers of silk, or taken
off course, caught in storms of thunder
currents or tides of snow, whether free
in cells of honey or free over tundra
plains or alive inside the hearts of living
trees, whether merely moments of inert
binding in the tight blink of buried
eggs, or a grip of watching in the cold
wick of water-swept seeds, this—beyond
faith, beyond doubt—we are here.

244

PATTIANN ROGERS

has published nine books of poetry; a book-length essay, *The Dream of the Marsh Wren;* and *A Covenant of Seasons,* poems and monotypes, in collaboration with the artist Joellyn Duesberry. Her most recent book, *Generations*, was published by the Penguin Group in 2004. *Song of the World Becoming: New and Collected Poems, 1981–2001* (Milkweed Editions) was a finalist for the *Los Angeles Times* Book Prize and an Editor's Choice in *Booklist*. The original *Firekeeper: New and Selected Poems* was a finalist for the Lenore Marshall Award and a *Publishers Weekly* Best Book of 1994. Rogers is the recipient of two National Endowment for the Arts grants, a Guggenheim Fellowship, and a poetry fellowship from the Lannan Foundation. Her poems have won the Tietjens Prize, the Bess Hokin Prize and the Frederick Bock Prize from *Poetry*, the Roethke Prize from *Poetry Northwest*, two Strousse Awards from *Prairie Schooner,* and five Pushcart Prizes. In May 2000 Rogers was a resident at the Rockefeller Foundation's Bellagio Study and Conference Center in Bellagio, Italy. Her papers are archived in the James Sowell Family Collection of Literature, Community, and the Natural World at Texas Tech University. Rogers has been a visiting professor at numerous universities and colleges and was an associate professor at the University of Arkansas from 1993 through 1997. She is the mother of two sons and grandmother of two grandsons and lives with her husband, a retired geophysicist, in Colorado.

Founded as a nonprofit organization in 1980, Milkweed Editions is an independent publisher. Our mission is to identify, nurture and publish transformative literature, and build an engaged community around it.

milkweed.org

INTERIOR DESIGN BY CHRISTIAN FÜNFHAUSEN

TYPESET IN REQUIEM HTF TEXT ROMAN